AN EDUCATORS GUIDE TO
DIFFICULT PARENTS

OTHER BOOKS BY JERRY WILDE

Hot Stuff to Help Kids Chill Out: The Anger Management
Book

Teaching Children Patience Without Losing Yours (with Polly
Wilde)

Why Kids Struggle in School: A Guide to Overcoming
Underachievement

Treating Anger, Anxiety, and Depression in Children and
Adolescents: A Cognitive-Behavioral Perspective

Anger Management in Schools: Alternatives to Student
Violence

Rational Counseling with School-Aged Populations: A Practical
Guide

Rising Above: A Guide to Overcoming Obstacles and Finding
Happiness

The Subject is Joy: A Path to Lifetime Contentment through
Value-Based Living (with John Wilde)

AN EDUCATORS GUIDE TO DIFFICULT PARENTS

JERRY WILDE, 1962 –

Kroshka Books
Huntington, New York

Editorial Production:	Susan Boriotti
Office Manager:	Annette Hellinger
Graphics:	Frank Grucci and Jennifer Lucas
Information Editor:	Tatiana Shohov
Book Production:	Patrick Davin, Cathy DeGregory, Donna Dennis, Jennifer Kuenzig, and Lynette Van Helden
Circulation:	John Bakewell, Lisa DeGangi and Michael Pazy Mino

Library of Congress Cataloging-in-Publication Data

An Educators Guide to Difficult Parents / Jerry Wilde.

      p.   cm.

    ISBN 1-56072-763-2

    1. Parent-teacher relationships—United States. 2. Interpersonal conflict. 3. Conflict management. I. Title.

LC225.3.W54   2000   99-055100

371.19'2--dc21   CIP

Copyright © 2000 by Jerry Wilde
    Kroshka Books, a division of
    Nova Science Publishers, Inc.
    227 Main Street, Suite 100
    Huntington, New York 11743
    Tele. 631-424-6682 Fax 631-424-4666
    e-mail: Novascience@earthlink.net
    e-mail: Novascil@aol.com
    Web Site: http://www.nexusworld.com/nova

Printed in the United States of America

CONTENTS

PREFACE

Let me warn you in advance, this is not your normal educational tome. It is not a book replete with empirical findings supporting the author's contentions. It was my mission to include exactly "zero" studies in this book and I succeeded. You've all read your share of research and have probably found it about as entertaining as watching grass grow. I've actually **done** my own and found conducting research is even less fun than reading about it.

This book is not overly concerned with political correctness. I'm just gonna tell it like it is and in the process, some readers may feel offended. Believe me, that's not my intent. I've been pretty good at offending people for a long time now and have never had to try very hard.

Your author has two simple goals: 1) Have some fun, maybe bring a smile to your face before the "worry wrinkles" become firmly entrenched and 2) pass on a few of the insights I've gained over the past ten years working with parents in schools. Simply put, I'd like to save you some of the pain I've endured. That's just the kind of humanitarian guy I am.

We'll start by examining the make-up of the difficult parent, known in Latin as "parentus painous buttockusk." Difficult parents can be broken down into two subtypes and we'll examine the similarities, differences, and motivations of each in turn.

There will also be an analysis of special education and Section 504 laws. The statutes change from state to state so this will be a general overview of the federal laws. However, I can provide some insights on what to do and NOT to do if your goal is to have a long career and live a happy life. Techniques for dealing with parent advocates will also be examined.

The components of successful parent conferences will be discussed along with an analysis of parental ownership. What should be the school's responsibility and what should stay with the parents? That's a very important question and often isn't given enough attention.

A hazard in this profession, job burnout, is also covered. The physical, emotional, and psychological warning signs are discussed along with measures that can be taken to prevent burnout.

Finally, techniques to understand and cope with anger and anxiety are provided. I'm not a legal expert but I'm fairly certain "choking someone" is still on the books as at least a misdemeanor in most states so you can cross that one off your list before we even start.

On a serious note, the work that you do with kids is very important. I know how exhausting and stressful it can be. And I also know that if we don't lighten up and keep things in perspective, we won't enjoy the journey we share with those kids. So on that note, put your feet up and relax. I sincerely hope you like this book.

Jerry Wilde
February 2000

Chapter 1

INTRODUCTION

S omeone had to write this book. I'm not sure I'm the person but the field of education can't wait any longer. The sky is on fire, there's lawlessness in the streets and more importantly, the toilets in 37.6% of all elementary school bathrooms are overflowing. Now if that isn't a sign of the apocalypse, what is?

This is a book that's long overdue. After all, there certainly aren't any classes in college on dealing with difficult parents. But there are enough "fluff" classes in educational coursework to keep a pillow factory well supplied until the above mentioned apocalypse does transpire. Whatever lessons educators have learned about difficult parents have been acquired through the experience of having our heads handed to us and/or having our behinds drop kicked. Come to think of it, maybe I am the person to write this book seeing as I haven't sat down with complete comfort since the Reagan administration.

Knowing how to deal with difficult parents is essential if you plan on having a career in education. Those of us in public education cannot turn the customers (i.e., the students and families) away like individuals in the private sector. I often ask my principal after a particularly difficult week, "Can we put up the 'no vacancy' sign?" The answer is, of course, "No." We have to deal with whomever shows up in our classrooms and offices on Monday morning. But that's okay because we're tough. Teaching is not for wimps.

There was a brief moment in my life when I was able to experience the joy of turning away a difficult client. As a psychologist I "moonlight" a few nights a week counseling adults. (Forty hours a week of abuse isn't enough for me.) I was conducting a drug and alcohol assessment with a client one evening because this individual had reached for a gun after a dispute with his wife! (No, I'm not kidding about this one.) During the assessment it came out that he had been arrested on two prior occasions for operating a motor vehicle under the influence of alcohol. He told me those two occasions were the only times he had used alcohol and driven. "Wow! That's bad luck," I thought. This client lived in the same town as his parents and brothers but hadn't spoken to his family in over ten years. In short, he was the kind of charismatic, witty, well-read intellectual you'd love to spend evenings with for the next six to eight months.

After the assessment he asked me, "So what do we do now?" I replied, "If you want to quit drinking, then you would come to see me. But you've made it very clear that you don't think you have a problem. You've got your assessment like the court ordered and **now you can leave**." What a great feeling. Just imagine if we could select a small percentage of emotionally disturbed parents, who seem to have it as their personal agenda to make our lives a living hell, and ask them to leave. Wouldn't it be great if life were actually like that!?! Reality check...it's not.

WHO IS THIS GUY ANYWAY?

It's not for me to judge whether I'm the person to write this book. Maybe a little background information about my family and I will help you decide. My oldest brother is a multi-millionaire who works less than sixty days a year. My next oldest brother is a very successful physician who lives in a house with slightly less square footage than the Astrodome. And then there's me...I work in schools.

I can't say they didn't try to warn me. They told me I'd be poor. They told me I wouldn't get any respect or appreciation. I told them I liked kids. They told me they liked kids, too, but that didn't mean they wanted to be poor, unappreciated adults. I told them I thought I'd make a good psychologist. They said nothing. After a long pause my doctor brother said, "That's great but I work with a lot of psychologists and they're all...crazy." I said, "Well, I've got that part covered already."

The above situation is all true. You can ask my brothers. The millionaire brother is always home and I think he now has a phone extension by his hot tub. I think of that sometimes when I'm shoveling down a "turkey surprise" hot lunch from the cafeteria. (The name comes from the fact that you'd be surprised if you knew what was in that turkey.)

I really am a school psychologist and I want you to know I've been there with you all. I've been at hundreds of late, late afternoon meetings that seem to drag on forever. I've been involved in numerous on-going battles with parents who seem to think "free and appropriate education" actually means "the finest educational support system available in this, or any other, galaxy." I've tried to explain to parents that their child's barking like a dog in the middle of a spelling test really *does* have an impact on the classroom environment. I've listened in a state of disbelief as a parent has tried to convince me that his child's choking another student was just a case of innocent mischief. I've wondered, as you have, who might have taught this little tike such an excellent "sleeper hold" to apply to his victims, I mean, classmates.

I realized it was time to write this book when I had become almost completely mentally numb. When you start asking things like, "Did that happen last fall?" and your colleague says, "No, that was four years ago." Once you are past the point of losing sleep over trauma, you're ready to write about it.

My introduction to the world of education was pretty unremarkable. I graduated with a specialist degree in education (BA + 60 credits) and decided I was sick of the Iowa winters. My wife and I decided to move to Arizona. I was 25, long on enthusiasm but short on skills, knowledge, and experience. I was going to be working for an assistant superintendent who had more than twenty years experience in education. In November of my first year, with three months as a professional under my belt, he called me into his office and told me he was quitting at the end of the week and moving back to Kansas. I was about to be promoted to director of special education. Let me assure you I was less than enthusiastic about this "battlefield promotion." In business, a promotion usually means much more pay, less work. In education, a promotion often means much more work, same pay (as it did in my case).

I guessed I wasn't ready for this position and, for a change, I was right. Looking back it was a good experience because it forced me to mature and learn even faster than I would have if my boss had stayed.

After two years in the desert I was ready to shovel snow again. We moved back to the Midwest but this time we settled in Wisconsin to begin life "Behind the Cheddar Curtain." Strange place, Wisconsin. The residents here seem to be especially proud of the fact that we lead the nation in obesity and alcohol consumption. In the immortal words of Dean Vernon Wormer from the movie *Animal House*, "Drunk, fat, and stupid is no way to go through life."

Let me just say, the state has its quirks. For example, when the University of Wisconsin football team makes a first down everyone in the entire state shows their joy by belching in unison. Wisconsin does have a fine educational system. The opportunity to go to school in Iowa and then practice in Arizona and Wisconsin has given me the chance to compare and contrast different ways of administrating special and regular education. I'm going to try and say this without sounding overly pejorative. Give me the Midwest!

My first job in Wisconsin was working two half-time jobs which turned out to be two full-time work loads. I did more than 140 psychological evaluations that year. For those of you who aren't versed in the appropriate number of evaluations per year, 140 is a lot. In fact, it's more than a lot. Anything over 125 falls into the official category of "shitload."

As you might have figured, I didn't stay in that job long. I moved down the road twelve miles and started working for a district whose psychologist was retiring after 30 years of pounding punishment. As they say, the third time is the charm. The staff and administration are great to work with and if I leave this job, it will be to do something completely different such as counsel charismatic, witty, and well-read intellectuals who pull guns on their spouses.

As I've traipsed around the country what I haven't gotten away from are the difficult parents. They're like a song by the Monkees that keeps running around in your mind all day. I once heard that the only way to get annoying songs out of your head is to sing them aloud. I thought the same principle might apply to difficult parents. By writing about the things I've learned, I might be less annoyed by the hassles they can cause.

SOME OF THIS WILL BE SERIOUS

I don't want you to be confused when I seem to be actually trying to communicate something important. I may just (accidentally) make a coherent point every so often. The intent of this book is to have some fun since we are all going to die penniless and unappreciated. At least we can learn something about the parents of the children that allow us to pay our mortgages. And maybe we'll have some fun along the way.

Chapter 2

UNDERSTANDING THE
DIFFICULT PARENT

This is a world filled with uncertainty with very few absolutes. Everything seems to have a shade of gray. One of the few certainties is that it's impossible to really fix something until you know what's wrong with it. Most people would agree with that supposition in principle but I often watch teachers trying to "fix" situations without first understanding the root of the problem. And believe me, I am by no means the first to observe this phenomenon. Henry David Thoreau said it best when he noted, *"For every thousand hacking at the leaves of evil, there is one striking at the root."*

With this in mind, this chapter will be devoted to unraveling the motivations driving difficult parents. Gaining a clear understanding is important because if you don't know where you're going or how to get there, you may be making "excellent time" on your journey but headed in the wrong direction. Wow...that seemed better in my mind than on the printed page and therefore I solemnly promise that will be my last attempt at a metaphor...or was that an analogy? I always confuse the two. Anyway...

I've thought about this quite a bit and have come to the conclusion that difficult parents can be broken down into two subtypes: 1) **The Real Mean Kind** and 2) **The Not-So-Mean But Pretty Darn Ineffective Kind**. Let's start with the Real Mean Kind.

THE REAL MEAN KIND OF PARENT

The most common motivation for these parents is the need to **project blame**. Let's face it, the parents we have the most contact with are the parents whose children are having some kind of difficulty. We'd all love to spend our time focusing on the children who are successful and fun to work with but that's just not the case. Think of it this way; if it weren't for the real mean kind of parent our jobs would actually be FUN. And if our jobs were fun, they wouldn't pay us because everybody would be willing to do it. Rejoice the existence of real mean parents because otherwise we'd all be living in the streets.

A large percentage of difficult parents are angry and looking to assign the blame to someone. This "someone" often winds up being a school employee, usually a teacher or administrator, who is supposedly treating the child unfairly.

Let me say before we go on that there are occasions where a teacher or school employee is out of line. I'm sure you've all seen instances where teachers **do** have it out for a student. For some reason they have lost their objectivity and treat a child unfairly. In a more extreme example, there are some teachers who don't like kids. Maybe they did at one time but not anymore. You know who I'm referring to because there are a couple in every district.

When it is a "teacher problem" and not a "student problem," the situation needs to be dealt with as quickly as possible for the sake of the child. Whether it is moving the student to another classroom or intervening with the teacher, care has to be given to make certain the student's welfare is protected. It's not really a fair fight between a fourth grader and a forty-five year old, is it? As a school psychologist I've been in the middle of a few of these "personality conflicts" and they are ugly. For the sake of everyone involved, it's best to try to deal with the situation quickly and move on.

BLAME REVISITED

Let's get back to parents projecting blame which is an all too common occurrence. Why is this such a common scenario in our schools and in society in general?

One of the reasons has to do with parents who confuse their parenting skills with their value as human beings. They can't make the distinction between who they are as people and who they are as parents. Parents overgeneralize from the idea that, "I am less than perfect as a parent" to the belief, "I am, therefore, a complete failure as a human being."

Everyone has some skills that are stronger than others. Some people are very talented artists and others can't draw stick people. Some are athletically talented or very skilled with computers. No one would deny these truths.

By the same token, some people are very good parents and others are not. The problem comes about due to the fact that everybody **thinks** they are good parents. I've yet to meet a parent who will say, "I'm really good at accounting but I suck at parenting." Why is there such self-delusion about parenting skills? This lack of awareness cannot be due to simple ignorance.

The answer is most adults can't admit they are having trouble parenting because they believe it is a sign of weakness, inferiority, and stupidity. Admitting you're less than adequate as a parent would be like saying, "I'm a useless tub of goo."

PROTECTING THE CHILD

Another motive for difficult parents (the real mean kind, that is) revolves around their need to protect the child at all costs. They believe it is the parents' job to make the child's life happy and free from any discomfort. Some have called these parents "helicopters" because they are always hovering around the child ready to drop in for the rescue.

This is not only troublesome to deal with as an educator but is unhealthy for the child. The unspoken message to the kid is, "You can't do anything on your own. I MUST watch out for you." Talk about setting the kid up for self-esteem problems later in life. These parents are programming their kids to be helpless and dependent. And usually, that's exactly how their kids turn out. These are the adolescents who can't make a decision. It's as if the umbilical cord is still connected...you just can't see it.

When the school tries to correct the child for even a slight error the kid learns to run home to mommy and daddy and the parents will tear up to school to rescue the student. I must admit I often think, "Oh well, I'm not the one creating this child and that kid won't be living at *my house* when he/she is 27." You reap what you sow...there's no way around it.

I've often thought these parents have the same effect on their children as cigarettes...they stunt the kids' growth. When I am dealing with these situations and feeling frustrated, I try to remind myself to stop and think it through. I usually end up feeling very sad for the child because he is the one that really loses out.

OVER IDENTIFICATION

Many difficult parents are hard to work with because they over identify with the child. It's as if the child were a part of them....a walking, talking extension of the father or mother. The parents look at the child and see a shorter, younger, thinner version of themselves.

All parents live vicariously through their children to a certain extent. That's only natural. However, these parents take it to an unhealthy extreme. When little Willie wins the mile race in fifth grade, it's as if Willie's father had actually crossed the finish line.

Often these parents did not have a happy childhood and want their kid's early years to be perfect. Hey, don't we all. When the school does anything other than continue to bolster the child's sense of well-being, the parents overreact. That's too soft of a word. They freak out.

PARENTS OF HANDICAPPED STUDENTS

The final group, in this subtype, are parents who have had the misfortune of having a child with a handicapping condition. As you know, exceptional educational need (EEN) students have many more rights than non-EEN students. As you probably also know, these parents can make your professional life very, very difficult.

They can request numerous IEP meetings that can be very time consuming. One year I had a parent who requested ten IEP meetings for his child. The problems come about due to the fact that you can't refuse to meet with parents if they request an IEP meeting. If they want to hold an IEP meeting to discuss some irrelevant point, you have to schedule a meeting. By the tenth meeting of the year, I would have preferred to be at the dentist having my teeth drilled...without the nitrous!

Occasionally you will come across a set of parents with a strong desire to hurt back. The tendency to want to lash out when you feel you have been treated unjustly is a normal human reaction. Parents of EEN students have been hurt in the worst way imaginable...by something happening to their child. Someone else is going to pay for that pain. It makes no difference that the school is an innocent bystander. Parents have the power to make the school jump through hoops and some use this endowment just for the sheer enjoyment of wielding power.

They confuse the important responsibility of being an advocate for their child with the opportunity to take as much as possible from the school whether or not it will benefit the student. Why do they want a nurses aide with the child at school? Because the law says they are entitled!

Sometimes it has little or nothing to do with what is in the best educational practices for their child. The school becomes the "bad guy" because, in the parent's subconscious, someone has to pay for their misfortune. Some parents of EEN students mistakenly believe they have earned the right to hurt others because they have been hurt.

Let me add that an overwhelming majority of parents of EEN students are very agreeable. They're great parents who are trying to look out for their child's best interests. It becomes hard when parents don't understand that the school also wants what is best for the child. A few times I've said to parents, "We (the school) aren't the enemy. We're part of the solution." If the parents hear that and understand it, things usually go smoothly. It is a very small percentage who use their power maliciously.

In one case the child's parents wanted the school district to hire a teacher of the hearing impaired for their child. The school didn't think that a full-time teacher was warranted because the child's needs could be met in a mainstreamed classroom part of the day. The parents weren't happy with this arrangement but agreed to give it a try.

The next problem came about due to the difficulty of finding a teacher of the hearing impaired. They aren't exactly sitting next to the phone waiting for someone to call. The market is such that teachers of the hearing impaired can pick from dozens of job offers.

We decided to expand our job search and go nationwide. We still weren't having any luck and the parents were getting increasingly angry. It seemed like the father called me every other day to check on the situation. They threatened to sue the school district to which I replied, "Okay." I don't think he liked that. Hey, I was young.

They didn't seem to understand that the school did not have the responsibility to kidnap someone and make them work for us. As long we were making a good faith effort to find a teacher (and we were) I wasn't worried about being sued. Even if they did sue us and win, what could the court do? I wasn't sure but I didn't think they could order a teacher to take training to become certified in case we couldn't recruit a certified teacher of the hearing impaired.

So far we've been discussing **The Real Mean Kind** of parents who are difficult mainly because they are vengeful. I also want to present some information on **Not-So-Mean But Pretty Darn Ineffective Kind** of parents who are enabling, inconsistent, and generally behave in ways that undermine academic pursuits.

EXPECTING FAILURE

Due to a lack of information and understanding, parents can unwittingly contribute to their child's school difficulties. Parents have a tremendous impact on the values, beliefs, and ideals of their children which, in some cases, is a shame. Whether they are aware of it or not, there is a continuous stream of information flowing out of parents communicating to their children. Students have an uncanny ability to read the subtle messages in this information. The wrong messages about school can have a negative effect on student's attitudes and, in turn, on their academic performance.

When there are difficulties at school often both parents and teachers experience irritation, frustration, and anger. When a child is capable of doing an adequate job in school but is not, every one is frustrated. It is easy for both parents and teachers to start blaming each other. The teachers say, "If the parents would give us some support, we could turn this student around. I only have her one period a day. After all, she's their kid." The parents say, "Why don't they teach the kid? That's what they get paid for. After all, she's their student."

Some of the parent's criticism of the school may very well be justified. The school might not be doing everything possible to guarantee a quality education for the child. However, this criticism should **not** be done in front of the student. When kids hear negative comments about education, it only reinforces their negative attitudes towards school. When a parent blames teachers for the child's difficulties, the student will believe it is the school's fault that she is failing. Magically, ownership for the problem is completely taken away from the child.

The truth is that if a child is failing, it is partially everyone's fault. The school and parents could probably be doing more to help. The student could certainly be doing more and eventually will have to do more if she is to improve. All three parties (the child, school, and parents) have a stake and it takes all three working together to be successful.

A perfect example of how blaming the school and backing the child can turn out to be a disaster occurred recently. A student was falling behind with his work in his sixth grade social studies class and was having to complete the work at home. He came to school one day and when the teacher asked for the assignment he had taken home, he claimed he had lost it. According to the student, he had the assignment in his coat pocket and it must have fallen out on the way home.

Even if that were true and the student did lose the assignment, the child is responsible for turning in the homework on time. The student protested that the teacher was being unfair. The teacher explained that the rules were very clear and simple. The punishment for not turning in an assignment was to spend one noon recess period in detention making up the missing work.

The next day the student brought a note from home which read in part, "You are being very unfair to my child. If he says he lost the assignment then I believe him. He shouldn't be punished for making an honest mistake. Are you (the teacher) perfect and have never lost anything accidentally? Do not punish my child for things that are beyond his control."

From that point on the student knew, right or wrong, the parent would back him and not his teacher. As you might have guessed, more assignments were lost and the consequences for such irresponsible behavior never really fell squarely on the shoulders of the student. I honestly believe that the parent did not realize the damage he was doing by unconditionally backing the student. The end result was the undermining of the teacher's authority and giving permission for the child to pick and choose which rules he was going to follow.

WATCH YOUR MOUTH!

Parents have to closely monitor what they convey about school because of the potential impact. The parents who suffered through school have basically two choices when it comes to what they are going to communicate to their children about school: 1) Parents can tell kids school was hard and they hated it. 2) Parents can tell their children school was hard but they wish they had tried harder. Often these parents realize that school was their ticket to a better life and even though school was not always fun, it was extremely important. I know you'll have no difficulties deciding which attitude will promote achievement and which will not.

Parents who openly express attitude # 1 are forgetting that their children closely identify with them. Children look up to their parents and often imitate their behavior. Well, that's true until they get to be teenagers and get tattoos and nose rings. Take that as an indication that they don't want to be like their parents anymore. When parents say, "I wasn't any good in school" they are laying the ground work for a son or daughter to follow in their footsteps. It is almost as if they are being given permission to perform poorly because there is an unspoken message that follows the initial statement, "I wasn't any good in school." The unspoken portion is, "And I don't expect you will be either." Students perceive the unspoken part just as clearly as if the parent had said it aloud.

EXPECTATIONS

Expectations are so important in predicting the success or failure of any endeavor. This is especially true in school. When students think they are going to succeed, they usually do. When they think they are going to fail, they usually do.

When parents and teachers set high but realistic expectations, students will try to meet those expectations. The same is true for low expectations. When you expect little, you'll receive diddly.

A fascinating process occurs that partially explains this phenomenon. When a student holds the belief, "I'm no good in school," he actually feels more comfortable if the results support that belief. That is, if a child expects to do poorly and does, he feels at ease with those results because failing is consistent with the expectations. When the results are inconsistent with the expectations there is a sense of uneasiness or even outright anxiety. When a student is used to getting "C's" and then receives the highest score in the class, it can be anxiety producing because the results don't support the core belief, "I'm no good in school." This phenomenon, known as **cognitive dissonance**, doesn't appear to make sense until the underlying dynamics are examined. Logically it would appear that any student used to getting "C's" would be thrilled to get the top score in the class.

Have you ever heard someone being described as "programmed to fail" - the type of person who is making great strides towards succeeding and at the last minute does something to completely mess things up? It's almost like they were trying to fail. The sad and peculiar thing is that they were subconsciously working towards failure. The anxiety produced by the inconsistency between the belief, "I can't do well" and the reality that they were about to succeed is overwhelming. They trip themselves up and return to a state where their beliefs match the results, namely failure.

It seems like it should be possible to simply *tell* students they are bright and can do well, and magically, their beliefs will change. The problem is that once they adopt a negative self-concept as learners, they reindoctrinate themselves with these beliefs literally hundreds of times a day. They tell themselves, "I can't do this" or "I'll never be able to understand fractions." This type of self-talk or internal dialogue occurs at a subconscious level most of the time. These self-talk "tapes" are buried but they play constantly. That's why it is so hard to change a negative self-concept once it has been established.

MEGAN'S STORY

There was a little girl, Megan, I had a chance to work with a few years ago. She was a very bright child with an IQ of 125 which is almost in the gifted or genius range. Her potential was greater than nine out of ten students her age and may have been even higher if it weren't for the fact that she had some learning problems. Megan was not a good reader and had a difficult time remembering things. She had other real strengths, however. She could understand verbal analogies better than most high school students even though she was in third grade.

Her parents asked if I could help them understand why school wasn't going as well as it could have been. They would go over and over her spelling words and she would still miss several on each test. They would study for a social studies exam and her father would swear that when she went to bed the night before the test, she knew all the information. She would somehow still do poorly on the exams.

After evaluating Megan, I sat down with her parents and explained that she did indeed have some memory problems that were probably interfering with her progress. I also suggested some techniques to help her more effectively remember what she had read. But the most important thing I did for Megan was to convince her she was a very bright little girl. I also told her that the types of activities they were doing in school would be changing. In a few years they would be expecting students to use skills such as logical thinking. I told her she was as smart as most high school students in these areas even though she was only in third grade. I also told her that I really, truly believed she was going to do much better and that eventually she would be one of the very top students in her grade.

A few years have passed and I did hear from Megan's parents recently. They said her grades had been steadily improving and that on the last report card she had earned straight "A's." They said the little hints I had given her about ways to improve her reading had helped her but that what really made the difference, in their opinion, was the talk I had with Megan. They said they could see that Megan really believed things would get better in the future and they did. Was this a fluke? I don't know for sure but I am convinced that whatever can be done to change a student's beliefs from, "I can't" to "I can" is worth trying. Nothing I know of will have a greater impact on a student than this change in attitude.

INCONSISTENCY

Inconsistency leads to a lot of difficulties with students. Some parents (and teachers) are inconsistent and aren't even aware of it. Inconsistencies give mixed messages to students which confuse them. Hopefully in this section we can examine a few ways to avoid inconsistency and the difficulties it can bring about.

WATCH WHAT PEOPLE DO,
NOT WHAT THEY SAY

People spend time and energy on things they deem important. If you really value having a sharp looking car, you spend time waxing and cleaning the car. If looking good at the beach is of vital importance to you, lifting weights and working out are probably part of your daily routine. If education is truly a top priority, parents probably spend time quizzing their kids for spelling tests, helping with homework, and numerous other activities that demonstrate that interest. Some parents talk about the importance of education but don't actually *do* anything to demonstrate their concern. Kids know the truth.

At report card time parents may give lectures about the importance of working hard in school and are probably sincere. However, nothing takes the place of daily involvement in their educational activities. It takes the daily demonstration of concern to really convince kids that education is a priority.

If parents value education and demonstrate this value, chances are their children will believe school is important as well. As has been emphasized, children identify with parents. They tend to value and believe in the same things their parents do. But it takes more than lip service. It takes real commitment.

Parents also act inconsistently by failing to follow through on promises. If parents state that homework time is every night from 7:00 - 8:00 p.m. and then two nights later let the child skip studying, what message are they sending?

OVER INVOLVEMENT

Occasionally a situation arises where parents become overly responsive to the needs of their son or daughter. The parents are so concerned and involved that their child's problems become the adult's problems.

The child learns that by sitting back and playing the victim, the parents will come to the rescue. If they wait long enough and continue to flounder, the parents will take over all the responsibility and basically do their school work.

A pattern is set up so when homework time comes, the child will start the assignment by looking confused briefly before stating emphatically, "I can't do this" or "I don't get it." The parent will help the child with a problem or two and say, "Now you do the rest." The child will wait the required 30 - 60 seconds with the obligatory puzzled look on his/her face before saying, "I still don't get it." The parent may do a few more problems and leave thinking the child surely understands now. Once again the child asks for assistance and this time the parent thinks, "Well, there's only eight left. I'll just help with the rest so I know he gets it." The problem is that the student really doesn't learn anything about the assignment but did learn a clever way of getting out of homework.

SUMMATION

This discussion of difficult parents is by no means exhaustive. I do, however, believe that most of the difficult parents we encounter in our professional lives fall somewhere in these categories. Now that we have a better understanding of their motives, we are in a better position to comprehend and deal with their antics. At least we are operating from wisdom rather than ignorance which is a better position, regardless of the particular circumstances.

Chapter 3

THE PARENTS' LEGITIMATE POWER

L et's cut right to the chase and say this clearly so everyone understands. **Parents have enormous power when it comes to the education of their children.** However, most don't know this.

For example, the law requires that parents be given copies of their rights under special education law, but an overwhelming majority don't actually take the time to read them. Even if they do look over the pamphlets we give them, do you think these rights are clearly understood? Parents understand school law about as well as I understand chemical engineering. So parents usually remain quiet to avoid asking the uncomfortable questions, just like we would in a class at MIT.

Most parents are more than reasonable and only want minor modifications made for the student. However, there are some parents who seem to derive pleasure from making our lives miserable (feel free to review the previous chapter if necessary). It's important to have an understanding of how educational laws work so schools can ascertain their chances of winning a legal battle or better yet, staying out of the courts altogether. With this in mind, we can turn our attention to special education and Section 504 (now would be a good time to take your No Doze if you have some.)

Before you start snoring, let me assure you that this will not be a detailed analysis of special education and 504 law. First off, you don't need to know the trivial details of these laws. Second off, even if you did have these laws memorized, the way the laws are written is much less important than the interpretation of the laws. These interpretations differ and 504 laws have not been "court tested" yet in many instances. Third off, I'm much to lazy to spend the hours it would take to properly research these topics. I have much, much better things to do like watch my fingernails grow.

FREE AND APPROPRIATE PUBLIC EDUCATION

To start with, all children are entitled to a "free and appropriate public education"(FAPE). The "free" part is pretty clear (i.e., if you're charging students to take a math class you should probably stop that) but the "appropriate" angle gets a lot more complicated. Some parents mistakenly believe the word "appropriate" means "the best education in this or any other galaxy."

I told you earlier about a family who had a child who was diagnosed as hearing impaired. The school did a tremendous job of trying to meet this child's needs even though we were located in a very remote part of the state. We were 90 miles from the nearest university and 30 miles from the nearest Wal-Mart! The special education staff, principal and several of the teachers involved took sign language classes. The district purchased "FM units" (at a cost of several thousand dollars) that helped the child hear the teacher's voice. We held meeting after meeting trying to make certain we could do everything possible to be ready for this little girl when she came to kindergarten.

This wasn't enough for the parents. They wanted the school district to hire a teacher of the hearing impaired. We explained that it would be difficult to attract such a highly trained professional to such a God forsaken corner of the earth but we agreed to try. We ran advertisements all across the southwest but couldn't attract anyone. The parents said we should offer a higher salary. We declined. They threatened to sue to which I said, "Okay but you should realize that the law doesn't give us the right to kidnap someone and make them work here." They found my flippant attitude less than amusing.

My point is that even when you go above and beyond what the law requires, some parents will want more. Learn to spot these parents early. Be very suspicious if one or both of them are lawyers.

Some believe that because they have the power to demand accommodations they *should* demand accommodations.

THE INDIVIDUALS WITH DISABILITIES EDUCATION ACT

IDEA requires that all public schools have a procedure in place to evaluate children suspected of having a disability. The most common referrals are for learning disability and speech/language handicap. I read somewhere that there are 13 possible disabilities under IDEA which means there are four that I can't think of at the time being.

1). Learning disability (LD)
2). Emotional or Behavioral disability (ED or BD)
3). Cognitive Disability (CD) - formerly known as mental retardation or mildly mentally handicapped
4). Speech/Language disability
5). Physically handicapped (PH)
6). Visually Impaired (VI)
7). Traumatic Brain Injury (TBI)
8). Autistic
9). Other Health Impaired (OHI)

These conditions all have various criteria to qualify and I'm not going to waste your time going over that because these change from state to state and, you guessed it, would be way too much work.

When a referral is made for an evaluation, the school district has a prescribed period of time to complete the evaluation, usually either 60 or 90 days. The child's parent or legal guardian must give written permission for the evaluation to be completed and can revoke this consent at any time.

LEAST RESTRICTIVE ENVIRONMENT

If the child meets the eligibility criteria and is found to be disabled in some way, there still needs to be a determination whether or not the handicapping condition is severe enough to warrant removal from regular classes. This requirement to educate children in as normal an environment as possible is known as Least Restrictive Environment (LRE). LRE states that a child *must* be educated in his or her regular classroom as much as is possible. Only when the handicapping condition is severe enough to significantly impact upon his or her educational progress can removal from this least restrict environment be considered.

MULTIDISCIPLINARY TEAM

This decision to remove a child from his or her regular classroom has to be made by members of a multidisciplinary team (M-team) which is composed of individuals who have completed some type of evaluation of the child. For example, in an LD referral, the M-team members would be the school psychologist, the educational programmer or LD teacher (who ever did the achievement testing), and the child's classroom teacher(s). When the various evaluations are completed and the reports are written, a meeting is held to determine whether or not the child meets the eligibility criteria of one or more of the handicapping conditions. If there is a difference of opinion by M-team members regarding the existence of a handicapping condition, the members of the minority opinion must state their reasons for disagreement in writing to the county director of special education or some other over paid big shot.

INDIVIDUAL EDUCATIONAL PLAN

If it is agreed upon by the members of the M-team that the child qualifies as handicapped, the law requires that the child have an Individual Education Plan...yes, the dreaded IEP. The law also requires that parents have input into the IEP even though some have difficulties spelling IEP. (Sorry, that was mean spirited and not necessary.)

The important thing to remember is that the IEP is a LEGALLY BINDING CONTRACT. Do not, I repeat, do not put anything in the IEP that you can not deliver. IEPs typically detail the goals that will be worked on while the child is receiving support services in the LD room. It also states the percentage of time that will be spent in the regular classroom and percentage in the LD class.

Time for another Arizona story, this one involving numerous IEPs. The folks out there wrote into each IEP of all the ED students they would receive weekly counseling. After the first week of school we were in violation of the IEPs on all ED students. Their intentions were good but their IEPs could have gotten our collective butts in a collective sling. It would have been much better to write something such as, "Student X will have the opportunity to work with the district's guidance counselor or psychologist if they choose to do so " or "on a 'as needed' basis."

Once the ink is dry on the IEP the parents still need to agree to the placement option the school district is offering. If the parents sign permission and thereby accept the program being offered they can still revoke their permission at any time and the child will be placed back into regular education.

If the child does not qualify for special education the parents can request a private evaluation and the school district must pay for the assessment. I have always felt this is completely unfair because the parents can select the evaluator. If the school has to pay for the evaluation I think the school should be able to give some selections of clinics and let the parents choose from the list.

The problem with allowing the parents to select the evaluator comes from the unethical practices of some private evaluation centers. Don't think I'm exaggerating when I tell you the psychologists at these clinics start their interview with the parents by saying, "What do you want the report to say?" They end the meeting with, "Tell the school to make the check payable to...." Yes, the parents are engaging in the fine tradition of "shopping for a diagnosis." The people operating these private clinics are engaging in the fine tradition of "driving expensive sports car."

Another problem comes about due to the fact that many of the psychologists at these clinics do not understand the educational criteria for a handicapping condition. When they use a phrase like "learning disability" they mean the child has some difficulties learning. The students still don't meet the eligibility criteria set up by the state but try explaining that to the parents after they've given you a report of the evaluation conducted by Dr. God. It puts the schools in an awkward position to say the least.

SECTION 504

Section 504, which has many similarities to IDEA, is a law that is *not* intended to have children removed from the regular class environment. Section 504 has actually been with us since 1973. Like Count Dracula, it has been waiting to be called forth to inflict fear and panic among the meek and pitiful (i.e., school employees). 504 has been used for years as a safeguard against employers discriminating against employees with disabilities. Within the last few years the Office of Civil Rights (OCR) has been using 504 to protect the rights of handicapped students. Once the advocacy organizations got wind of Section 504, it was targeted for use with children in schools.

Section 504 is enforceable in all districts that receive federal money. Like IDEA, Section 504 requires identification, evaluation, provision of appropriate services, and procedural safeguards in every public school in the country.

All students who are disabled under IDEA would also be handicapped under 504. However, the reverse is not necessarily true. A student suffering from asthma may be eligible for 504 modification but may not meet the requirements to be eligible under IDEA criteria.

The IDEA defines as eligible only students who have certain disabilities and who, because of the condition, need special education (specially designed instruction). Section 504, on the other hand, protects all handicapped students, defined as having any physical or mental impairment that substantially limits one or more of the major life activities.

Section 504 determines major life activities to include:

1) walking
2) seeing
3) hearing
4) speaking
5) breathing
6) learning
7) working
8) caring for oneself
9) performing manual task

One other important distinction regarding 504 has to do with the coverage of students who may not actually have a handicapping condition but are "regarded as handicapped by others." I have no formal proof but I'm sure there are several people who regard me as having some type of handicap in one of those areas. In accordance with 504 law I would not want to be removed from my normal work environment so the only accommodation I'd like would be a hot tub installed in my office.

The handicapping condition need only substantially limit one major life area in order for the student to be eligible. Most of us are still waiting for the courts to define, in judicial terms, words like "substantial." If taken in a broad sense, some believe that 504 could include one out of every three students in school today.

It would cover things like the obese kids who have a difficult time in physical education (PE). In this case the schools would have to evaluate the child to determine whether or not he or she is eligible under 504. If so, school professionals would need to meet and draw up an accommodation plan which is similar to an IEP. The modifications would have to made in the child's PE programming.

It appears as though the biggest source of referrals will come from parents of children who have been diagnosed with attention deficit-hyperactivity disorder (ADHD). The advocacy group for ADHD kids known as C.H.A.D.D (which stands for "Children Held Accountable....Don't-u-Dare!) has used 504 to force schools to make accommodations for ADHD kids.

A percentage of ADHD kids already receive services under IDEA as either LD, ED or other health impaired (OHI). IDEA has the stipulation that the handicapping condition must be severe enough to warrant removal from the regular classroom. 504 does not.

If a kid walks into your building with a report from some doctor from somewhere, even if all the school professionals do not believe the child is ADHD, you are probably going to have to serve the child under 504. Thank you OCR! I know I can speak for all the public school employees everywhere when I say it's a good thing 504 came along when it did because we were running out of things to do!

When we have time to get out from under the pressures of gangs, school violence, truancy, high drop out rates, adolescent drug use and general chaos we're thrilled to have another gigantic "time suck" on our hands courtesy of the folks at OCR. Anyway, enough complaining from me. I think it might be helpful to compare and contrast 504 and IDEA.

GENERAL PURPOSE

IDEA - Is a federal funding statute whose purpose is to provide financial aid to states in their efforts to ensure adequate and appropriate services for disabled children.

504 - Is a broad civil rights law which protects the rights of individuals with handicaps in programs and activities that receive federal financial assistance from the U.S. Department of Education.

WHO IS PROTECTED?

IDEA - Identifies all school-aged children who fall within one or more specific categories.

504 – Identifies all school aged children as handicapped who meet the definition of handicapped as 1) has or 2) has had a physical or mental impairment which substantially limits a major life activity, or 3) is regarded as handicapped by others.

RESPONSIBILITIES

a) IDEA - Requires a written IEP with specific content and a required number of specific participants at the IEP meeting.

a) 504 - Does not require an IEP but does require an accommodation plan. It is recommended that the district document that a group of persons knowledgeable about the student convened and specified the agreed upon services.

b) IDEA - "Appropriate education" means a program designed to provide "educational benefit." Related services are provided if required for the student to benefit from specially designed instruction

b) 504 - "Appropriate " means an education comparable to the education provided non-handicapped students, requiring that reasonable accommodations be made. Related services, independent of any special education services as defined by IDEA, may be the reasonable accommodation.

SPECIAL EDUCATION VS. REGULAR EDUCATION

IDEA - A student is only eligible to receive IDEA services if the M-team determines that the student is disabled under one or more of the specific qualifying conditions and requires specially designed instruction to benefit from education.

504 - A student is eligible so long as he or she meets the definition of handicapped as 1) has or 2) has had a physical or mental impairment which substantially limits a major life activity or 3) is

regarded as handicapped by others. It does NOT require that the handicap adversely affect educational performance.

FUNDING

IDEA - Provides additional funding for eligible students.
504 - Does not provide additional funding. IDEA funds may not be used to serve children eligible only under 504.

ACCESSIBILITY

IDEA - Requires that modifications must be made if necessary to provide access to free and appropriate education.
504 - Has regulations regarding building and program accessibility, requiring that reasonable accommodations be made.

PROCEDURAL SAFEGUARDS

Both require notice to the parent with respect to identification, evaluation and/or placement.

a) IDEA - Requires written notice.
a) 504 - Does not require written notice but a district would be wise to do so.
b) IDEA - Delineates required components of written notice.
b) 504 - Not required.
c) IDEA - Requires written notice prior to any change in placement.
c) Requires notice only before a "significant change" in placement.

EVALUATION

a) IDEA - A full comprehensive evaluation is required, assessing all areas related to the suspected disability. Requires an M-team.

a) 504 - Evaluations draws on information from a variety of sources in the area of concern. Decisions are made by a group knowledgeable about the child.

b) IDEA - Requires informed consent before an initial evaluation is conducted.

b) 504 - Does not require consent, only notice.

c) DEA - Requires reevaluations at least every three years.

c) 504 - Requires periodic reevaluations. IDEA schedule for reevaluations will suffice.

d) IDEA - Reevaluation is not required before a significant change in placement. However, a review of current evaluation data is strongly recommended.

d) 504 - Reevaluation is required before a significant change in placement.

e) IDEA - Provides for independent evaluation at district expense if parent disagrees with the evaluation conducted by the school.

e) 504 - No provision for evaluations at district expense.

PLACEMENT PROCEDURES

Both laws require districts to:

a) Draw upon information from a variety of sources.
b) Assure that all information is documented and considered.
c) Ensure that all eligibility decisions are made by a group of persons including those who are knowledgeable about the child.
d) Ensure that the student is educated with his or her non-handicapped peers to the maximum extent possible (least restrictive environment).

IDEA - An IEP review meeting is required before any change in placement.

504 - A meeting is not required for any change in placement.

GRIEVANCE PROCEDURES

IDEA - Does not require a grievance procedure, nor a compliance officer.

504 - Requires districts with more than 15 employees to 1) designate an employee to be responsible for assuring district compliance with Section 504 and 2) provide a grievance procedure for parents, students, and employees.

DUE PROCESS

Both statutes require districts to provide impartial hearings for parents or guardians who disagrees with the identification, evaluation or placement of a student.

IDEA - Delineates specific requirements.

504 - Requires that a parent have an opportunity to participate and be represented by counsel. Other details are left to the discretion of the local school board.

ENFORCEMENT

a) IDEA - Enforced by the U.S. Office of Special Education Programs. Compliance is monitored by the State Department of Education and the Office of Special Education Programs.

a) 504 - Enforced by the U.S. Office of Civil Rights.

b) IDEA - The State Department of Education Resolves disputes.

b) 504 - State Department of Education has no monitoring, complaint resolution or funding involvement.

So you see, similar yet with some important differences. Please be advised that each state's interpretation of special education laws is different and the above descriptions are overviews taken from the federal laws regarding IDEA. Good luck!

Chapter 4

DEALING WITH ADVOCATES

If you were born under the right sign, or have led a life firmly entrenched in the "straight and narrow", or if you just happen to be lucky, you may have had very few dealings with parental advocates. Thank God now and often here after because this could change. You could be up to your arm pits in advocates soon and thinking back to your previous happy existence with teary eyed wistfulness.

Why can advocates create such problems? There are a few who have the knowledge of an infant but the teeth of the hydra. Most of the advocates I've worked with are parents of children who were born with handicaps. As was discussed earlier, a certain percentage of these parents have a strong desire to hurt something or someone because of their child's misfortune. Because they have experienced misfortune in life, someone else deserves to be punished. This "someone else" often winds up being the school because it is such an easy target. When the school will not provide their child with an individual tutor for note taking, the educational institution becomes "the enemy." These parents lose their perspective with regards to "reasonable accommodations" because they are so emotionally involved. I happen to know just enough about brain functioning to be dangerous. I'd like to apply that knowledge in an attempt to help you understand the dynamics at play in this situation.

A VERY SHORT LESSON IN NEUROPSYCHOLOGY

The sections of the brain that control higher level thinking are the frontal lobes. Take a guess where the FRONTal lobes are located. Good job. The emotional center of the brain is in an area known as the limbic system which has many connections with the frontal lobes. When neurons in the limbic system are firing rapidly (i.e., when people are very emotional) the controls of the frontal lobes are overridden. That's why people act like such fools when they are upset. (This may be of little or no interest to you but I've been studying neuropsychology for a long time now and it isn't very often I can work it into conversation so thank you for letting me indulge myself with a bit of a tangent. I'll try to keep these sidebars to a minimum.)

WHAT'S THE MOTIVE?

Most of us who have lived long enough realize there is very little, if any, altruism. Even when people are nice for no apparent reason, there is an incentive. We may not be able to see it. And the last time I checked, advocates were people too so that means they must be getting something out of this as well.

Some get paid so it is no mystery why they are adopting the role of advocate...it's for the good of the kids. (You can all start humming "God Bless America" at this point.) But most do not get reimbursed for their time so it must be something else.

It could be that they really have nothing better to do with their time. In today's world, where most people are scrambling to find time to get dressed and eat, it's important to realize there are people who are bored silly. But why is it that a lot of these people choose to occupy their time with creative pursuits that either intentionally or unintentionally annoy the heck out of the rest of us? I propose a solution to this problem. WE NEED MORE BOWLING LEAGUES!!!!

The other explanation has to do with the pleasure some people get out of being a pain in the behind. I do believe **these are the kind**

of advocates we all want to avoid because, as has been pointed out, the parents have a great deal of power on their side. If they have an advocate who knows how to be a professional fly in the ointment, they can waste a lot of our time and energy.

But lets get back to the advocate. Where do they come from? How does one become an advocate? And is it true that if you voted for Ronald Reagan you are an accomplice in his crimes against children? (Sorry, I promise that will be the last sidebar of the chapter. Feel free to replace "Reagan" with a "Clinton" if you prefer.)

As was stated previously, most advocates are parents who have had experience dealing with the school system through their own children. Many feel that the schools are not doing the right thing (or enough of the right thing) for kids so they decide to become professional advocates. The problem is they get very little training to help understand the swirling quagmire that is educational law. As I always say to my internship students, "If you don't understand educational law now, don't worry because it will be very different by this time next year."

Despite the fact that most advocates have very little training, they are sent forth to make schools provide for the educational needs of children. Sometimes their lack of training isn't detrimental because they realize they don't really understand the law and decide the best thing they can do is just be supportive to the parents. There was some beautiful quote, I believe by Mark Twain, that stated, "*It is better to remain silent and thought a fool than to speak and remove all doubt.*" Even if Mark Twain didn't really say it, the adage sounds an awful like something he might have said.

RETIRED PROFESSIONALS

Some advocates are retired professionals. This type is much more difficult to deal with because unlike the parents, they usually know the laws very well. Although this is not always the case either.

One of my earliest experiences with an advocate was with a retired professor from the University of Arizona. I was quite nervous, not because I believed the school was in the wrong, but because I had visions of F. Lee Bailey sitting down across from me.

As it turned out, the gentleman was woefully behind the times regarding changes in the law. I can't recall the particulars of the case but he asked for something to be done that pertained to some special education statute but the law had been changed years earlier. I was shocked that this former professor of special education hadn't heard about this change in the law. But then again, it was a PAC 10 school so I guess I should have expected as much. (Honest, that will be the last shot at the left coast schools for the remainder of this book.)

Be careful when you are dealing with a former professional. They can make things a lot more difficult for the school. And what's wrong with professionals advocating for kids? Nothing. I have no problems with advocates who know what they are talking about. In fact it probably keeps the school on their toes and makes certain the kids won't be short changed. Let's face it, there are schools out there doing the wrong thing. Some folks aren't interested in the welfare of kids as much as they are interested in the ease of their life. If, dear reader, this is you, shame, shame!

There have been times where I have been asked by friends to be a consultant or advocate for their child. I am more than happy to explain the laws to parents and give them my advice because I know schools can look the other way or make it difficult on parents.

There is the proverbial "code of honor" in some professions that means even if someone is doing something highly unethical, other professionals in that field should **not** be the whistle blower. If doctors learn of a ill advised practice by a colleague, some will not share their concerns with the patient due to potential repercussions from the doctor in question.

This is wrong. No matter how you slice it, this practice is unethical and frankly, reprehensible. Unfortunately, some educators also fall into this custom albeit to a lesser degree.

If someone is advising parents untruthfully or incorrectly, let the parents know the correct information. Maybe then we won't need advocates in the schools to police our actions because we are able to scrutinize ourselves.

I had been hearing some disconcerting news regarding a neighboring district's practices with parents. The parents said the district had told them they *had* to sign permission papers to put their child in special education or the student couldn't come back to school. At first I thought it was the parent's misunderstanding. It's not uncommon for parents to become confused at a meeting so I assumed that is what had happened. But then I heard a similar story from another parent...and another.....and another.

These kids kept showing up on our doorstep because the parents didn't want them in special education but obviously the school did. I know I sound like I am not in favor of advocates (and I'm usually not) but do you think the school would try this type of illegal behavior with an advocate at the meeting? Yes, Virginia, there is a need for advocates in some districts.

However, some advocates seem to believe their job is to push the school to do EVERYTHING for the child. That is not advocating...that is enabling. Most of these advocates are some type of mental health worker who is trying to keep the parents happy and keep the child in therapy (at $120 an hour.) These advocates know that what the parents often want is to not be bothered by school problems. The more the school handles, the less the parents are forced to deal with. All this translates, in a very complicated algebraic equation, into another Lexus for the advocate.

I have no respect for these folks as they are the worst kind of professional advocate...the kind that know better but do the wrong thing to appease the parents. A true advocate tries to find the proper balance between the responsibilities of the school, parents AND the child. One goal all schools have for kids is to foster independence. If the parents keep insisting that the school should take care of all problems for the child, how is the child ever going to learn to be self-reliant? Answer...they won't.

ADVOCATE TRAINING AND FUNDING

Another type of advocate is the weekend trained advocate who is armed with a little bit of knowledge. Often they do not realize how much they do not know. One instance comes to mind when an advocate made a long range prediction about a child going to college and what she would be like several years in the future. As it turns out she had met the student only an hour earlier! Clearly, this case was very complicated and had been going on for several years but this advocate thought she knew the answers to all our questions after spending a few minutes with the child. Her talents were obviously being misused as an advocate. She should have been in a shack on Coney Island with a crystal ball or at the very least reading palms at a circus somewhere.

Some of you may not realize that **our tax dollars go to support some of these advocacy groups**. The public tax dollar provides money for training and materials. While I'm not in favor of a lot of the cuts that are taking place in Washington these days, here is one program that could use a little trimming.

STRATEGIES

Time to turn our attention to strategies for dealing with advocates. The first advice is the simplest to carry out and that is to not a make an issue over the presence of an advocate at a staffing. I do think it is a good idea to introduce them at the meeting just to make certain if anyone came in late to the meeting they are aware there is a parent advocate present. Usually, it's obvious anyway. Some of these advocates couldn't be more conspicuous if they had police cherries spinning around on top of their fedoras.

Often they just sit and observe the meeting and do not add a lot. That's fine. Carry on with your meeting as planned. If parents feel better having them in the room, that's shouldn't be a problem for the school.

CHALLENGE CREDIBILITY

Problems start when they start speaking like an authority. When this happens, depending on your mood, you may want to challenge their credibility. By this I mean, ask them about their background. Let me give you an example.

Advocate: Don't you think Sara qualifies as learning disabled?
School: Excuse me, Mrs. Johnson, are you a school psychologist?
A: No.
S: Are you a specialist in learning disabilities?
A: No but my son was in an LD program.
S: But you've never had an formalized certification by the state as a learning disabilities instructor?
A: No, but I have been trained by the Professional Advocacy Group.
S: Have you ever taught?
A: No, but like I said I was trained.
S: And that training was for how long? Two years? Four years?
A: No, we were trained on two weekends.
S: Mrs. Johnson, that may seem like a lot of time but the professionals around this table have a minimum of a high school diploma, four years of college, and a master's degree in special education. Beyond that they have spent literally thousands of hours working in a professional capacity with children. I don't mean this to sound rude, but you don't have the training or experience to make the diagnosis of a learning disability.

After I do that I usually feel just a little bit guilty because it really is not done with the intention of being mean. But having a weekend advocate sit and discuss educational issues with a group of professionals is akin to educators discussing heart surgery. ("Well, no I never went to medical school but I had an uncle that *had* open heart surgery.")

Some professional advocates just don't realize how out of place they are. They do not deserve to be ridiculed, but parents often don't realize the advocate doesn't know what he or she is talking about.

Some advocates won't be discouraged after you've pointed out to them that they really don't know the intracacies of the law and will keep spouting off with their two cents worth. (Could it be that they themselves have a learning disability? Think about it.) When you come into contact with advocates who are difficult to discourage it can be a good idea to point out to the team around the table that Mrs. Johnson is free to participate in the meeting but that her comments should be taken as those of essentially a lay person and not as those of a professional.

I know colleagues who will use a great deal of educational and psychological jargon in an attempt to silence the advocate but I wouldn't recommend this. If you've got an advocate that doesn't get the point after trying the above two techniques, they simply aren't going to get the point. And since it would be in questionable judgment to tell them to "put a sock in it" it's best to simply smile and move forward.

That's not to say you should let them dominate the meeting. If necessary, you may have to dispute every point they bring up. Some parents will take your silence as agreement with the advocate so make certain the school's point of view is clear to all present.

PREVENTING THE BUSHWHACK

One final point, when you schedule a meeting with the parents it's not a bad idea to get into the habit of asking if they know who will be attending the meeting. They don't have to tell you this but they often will. If they say, "I am not required to let you know in advance who will be attending" you might as well set out an extra chair for the advocate. You can bet your bottom dollar one will be showing up after a response like that. Knowing in advance an advocate will be attending may help you make certain all your ducks are in a row.

Finally, I want to make it clear that I am not opposed to advocates if they know the law and are honestly try to support the parents. I don't appreciate it when the advocates sole motives is to be difficult. If the advocates agenda is to make certain the child gets the best education possible, then there is no reason to be alarmed...unless the school is doing something illegal. Then I'm glad that you're uncomfortable because the advocate is actually serving a purpose.

I do get annoyed when parents feel a need to bring an advocate because what that communicates to me is they don't trust our school. Somewhere along the way they got the feeling we wouldn't do the right thing or the best thing for their child. They do not realize that **our primary responsibility is to be an advocate for their child**. When they bring an advocate, we often feel like the school has let them down.

As I've said to parents before, "I didn't get into this line of work to take advantage of children. I could have done anything and I CHOSE to do this because helping kids is an important job." We need to also keep in mind that what we feel is right and what the parents think is right can be two entirely different things. With this in mind, maybe we shouldn't feel so frustrated when they come armed with an advocate. Perhaps these cases are merely the result of an honest difference of opinion.

Chapter 5

Burnout: Are You At Risk?

The title of this chapter is somewhat misleading. Burnout is probably a misnomer because it seems to insinuate that a single event caused the feelings that often accompany this type of emotional, physical, and spiritual exhaustion. Perhaps "rust out" or "wear out" would be more accurate because this phenomenon does not occur suddenly. In fact, it is usually insidious. You don't know how but eventually the fire in your belly is gone. It happens to thousands of us every year. Maybe some of the ideas in this chapter will keep you from being another casualty.

The subtitle of this chapter (Are You At-Risk?) isn't necessary. If you work as an educator, you are at-risk of becoming burned out. Any profession that puts a person in close contact with people all day is a high burnout field. It just goes with the territory.

If you've decided to read this book it probably means you've had more than your fair share of contact with difficult parents. Nothing can make another profession seem so appealing as difficult parents. There have been times I've muttered under my breath, "There's got to be an easier way to make a living." This usually follows a two hour IEP meeting or a day filled with phone calls from irate parents.

Let's move on to the most commonly occurring symptoms of burnout. Later in the chapter there will be recommendations to follow if you recognize some of these behaviors and attitudes in yourself.

SYMPTOMS OF BURNOUT

A.   Some of the general signs include:
1. Declining efficiency, works long hours and then takes on more work, displays poor judgment.
2. Mechanical functioning, decreased initiative and problem solving skills, capacity to make decisions impaired.
3. Decreased interest in work and loss of motivation.
4. Decreased quality of work. May feel they are not getting through to staff or students.
5. Decreased tolerance to the frustrations of ordinary or stressful situations (not able to handle situations as they usually would), avoidance of complicated or draining problems.
6. Questioning the value of oneself, peers, job and life.
7. Subjective feeling of exhaustion, worthlessness, helplessness, resignation, fear, anger, guilt, embarrassment, despair, being squeezed
8. Emotional withdrawal or avoidance of peers and family/friends, feels isolated.
9. Fantasies of escape, retaliation, or suicide. Unusual self-depreciating fantasies (giving up one's life for something)
10. Strong denial of the problem itself or its severity.

B.   Psychosomatic/Physical symptoms
1. Fatigue and exhaustion
2. Depression and anxiety
3. Headaches/migraines
4. Weight loss, loss of appetite
5. Insomnia
6. Shortness of breath
7. Hypertension
8. Difficulty relaxing
9. Loss of sexual drive
10. Ulcers, bowel difficulties, etc.

C.   Psychosocial/Behavioral symptoms

1. Mood swings, increased rigidity & negativity, decreased tolerance of ambiguity, feels unappreciated by peers and supervisors.
2. Change in regular pattern of behavior, becomes unreliable and stubborn, may perceive students simply as "problems" or difficult to manage.
3. Increased irritability, looks and acts depressed, inappropriate or displaced anger.
4. Suspiciousness, paranoid ideas, blames others for pressuring them, feels others may be out to get them.
5. Increased inappropriate risk taking with students and in one's personal life. Sexual acting out.
6. Compensating omnipotence and grandiosity.
7. Increased illness and absence from work.
8. Disorganized behavior, late to work, slow in completing work.
9. Diminished social and recreational interests.
10. Inability to enjoy normal pleasures or accomplishments.
11. Self-medication with alcohol, tranquilizers, sleeping pills, or uppers/downers.

TWO MAIN PREDISPOSING PERSONALITY TYPES

A.   Overly Conscientious Type
1. Moral, dedicated.
2. Strong desire to help.
3. Excessive empathy leads to increased giving to others and less for self.
4. Overly high expectations of self, compensates for hidden feelings of inadequacy.

B. Guilt Motivated Type
1. Overly responsible for other people and overly apologetic.
2. Drawn to give to make up for something.
3. The more this type has, the more they feel they have to make up for.

C.   Both Types Tend To:
1.   Deny their own feelings.
2.   Have a great need for approval.
3.   Need to feel indispensable.
4.   Have trouble setting appropriate limits and expectations.
5.   Use work to make up for what may be missing from ones' personal life and over identify with students.
6.   Have similar belief systems
   a.   Trust only yourself.
   b.   Others should see the world as they do.
   c.   Need to succeed no matter what.

CAUSATIVE FACTORS

A.   Work related
1.   Increased work load (more hours, difficult problems, holding more than one job).
2.   Decreased supervisor support of excessive responsibilities.
3.   Boredom due to repetitious tasks.
4.   Unclear limits of professional responsibilities.
5.   Loss of peer involvement or support.
6.   Promotion leading to stressful higher expectations for self.
7.   Lack of recognition or promotion, disappointment over unmet expectations.
8.   Insufficient time off, vacations, etc.

B.   Personal
1.   Withdrawal from family due to an over committed work schedule which leads to a loss of ones' family as a source of support.
2.   Losses or disappointments.
3.   Family changes or conflicts.
4.   "Middle age" crisis (a re-evaluation of what is important to you.)
5.   Personal illness or chronic illness in ones' family.

6. Lack of sufficient social & recreational activities/construction of areas of interest.

DEALING WITH BURNOUT

A. Friendly confrontation to discuss the need to address fatigue (i.e., burnout)
B. Be reassuring by identifying strengths, past successes and positive involvements.
C. Give permission to have burnout feelings and identify and discuss the normal signs/symptoms of burnout.
D. Get the person to take some time off and appreciate the need to meet ones' own needs and develop a plan to establish a balance in ones' personal life.
E. Set reasonable expectations for self and appropriate limits with others.
F. Decrease work load, providing peer support and decreasing boredom by sharing routine repetitive chores.
G. Increase regular time off and vacations.
H. Develop increased family involvement and support.
I. Develop hobbies and other rewarding recreational and social activities.
J. Develop a supportive "sponsor" relationship as part of a structured support system.

PREVENTION

A.   Professionally
   1. Improve team support and sharing of frustrations.
   2. Rotate tasks, diminish isolation.
   3. Recognize staff needs and resentments, initiate a good feedback system that recognizes success.
   4. Limit work hours and take regular time off.
   5. Provide adequate professional education and growth.

B.   Personally
1. Identify and review needs and goals, be optimistic.
2. Meet ones needs by balancing ones involvement with family/friends and social/recreational activities and regular physical exercise.
3. Practice complimenting yourself, positive self-affirmations.
4. Allow increased dependence on people close to you who make you feel good. (To compensate imbalance from being isolated until balance is restored.)
5. Learn to say "no" (set limits).
6. Give yourself "decompression time" after work on the way home or at home before getting involved with family members (walk, talk with a friend, rest, be alone), GIVE YOURSELF SOME SPACE.
7. Invest energy in trying to find a sense of achievement in whatever you undertake.

Here are some tips:

1. Start your day with some meditation, exercise or activity that is non-work.
2. Prepare yourself mentally on the way to work. Don't rehash what went wrong yesterday. Stay in the "here and now." Focus on what is ahead to accomplish. This will put you in the "mode."
3. Take regular breaks. You should have a few minutes twice a day to relax. DO NOT use this time in conjunction with work related activities (phone calls, short meetings, etc.)
4. Take a lunch. Not a working lunch. A lunch. If possible, leave the facility. If not, find a quiet place or share lunch with a colleague. Try to avoid work related discussions. Make this personal discussion time.
5. Budget your time. Make allotments for phone calls and correspondence. Make the schedule "flexible".
6. DON'T TAKE YOUR WORK HOME. On your way home, use the time to unwind. When you get home, make some time for you to relax (read, music, exercise). This may not work

for you but I will stay at the school until 5:00 p.m. as opposed to bringing work home with me. My time at home is for my family.

I have also learned to mutter, "I guess some of this isn't going to get done." I work very, very efficiently but crises do arise and we can either drive ourselves crazy because we won't be able to meet a deadline or accept the fact that sometimes the best laid plans fall apart due to unforeseen circumstances. Keep in mind that we all get panicked at times during the year because we have so much to do and so little time to do it. And somehow it all ends up getting done one way or another.

As my father used to say after I would describe some "horror" to him, "I'll bet you the sun will still come up in the East tomorrow." Guess what? My dad hasn't been wrong yet.

Chapter 6

DEALING WITH ANGER

L et's face it...most of you bought this book because the unrealistic
and unreasonable demands of parents are driving you crazy.
You're sick and tired of parents expecting champagne when you're
operating on a beer budget. In fact, it's starting to tick you off.
You've got a million and one things to do and no time for the
nonsense from a handful of parents. To be completely blunt about it,
these parents are *making you mad*. This only makes sense because
anger comes from insensitive people and unfair circumstances.
Right? Not exactly.

WHAT CAUSES ANGER ANYWAY?

It may come as a surprise to some but anger is not caused by
frustration as many so called experts proclaim. Anger (and its
partner, rage) comes from our personal philosophies and beliefs
about the world. In short, *anger comes from the demand that we not
be frustrated*. For example, being stuck in traffic does not *cause*
anger. Demanding that we not be stuck in traffic produces the type of
thinking that brings about the feeling of anger.

Wouldn't it be possible to be delayed by traffic and not be angry?
There have probably been times when we have been stuck in traffic
and not really minded. Maybe we're headed somewhere we'd rather
not be (like the opera or dentists office) and are in no hurry to get
there. In that case, we don't mind being a few minutes late. Perhaps

we are enjoying the company of a friend and the traffic delay merely prolongs the conversation. Maybe you just unwinding after a tough day and a few extra minutes in the car helps clear your head. The point is, being struck in traffic is basically *neutral* since it can bring about numerous emotions such as anger, boredom, irritation, distress and/or indifference.

Now if we're rushing home from work on Friday and traffic is backed up, we can make ourselves quite angry. The important point here is the event (being stuck in traffic) is exactly the same but people feel differently depending on their thoughts. If an event caused feelings, how could the same event cause different emotions? Logically, it could not, so the feelings must be created by something other than being stuck in traffic. In actuality, the emotion is created our beliefs/values/philosophies ABOUT being stuck in traffic. In effect, we are angry because of our demands.

The crazy thing about most anger is that your rage will have no impact on the situation. A person's anger is not going to make the traffic move any faster.

What about situations in which anger can be productive and assists us in getting what we want? There are situations in which anger can help people manipulate others in order to produce the results they desire. Some people are experts at intimidating others by displaying extreme emotions.

It's also a release to get really anger and vent that rage. Often people who are frustrated will tell you it feels good to really blow their top. Once they have vented some of their "righteous anger" they believe it is out of their system.

THE FALL-OUT FROM ANGER

Continually venting anger can bring about problems. People resent being mistreated and manipulated. Who can blame them? They may obey your demands but afterwards they'll retaliate, maybe not directly, but they won't forget.

Think of the last time someone jumped all over you for making a mistake. (If you are an administrator you may have to think back to your teaching days on this one or remember the last time a parent chewed you out over the phone.) If you're like most folks, you've probably corrected the mistake but you haven't forgotten the feeling of being ridiculed. If people make it a habit of bullying others, it takes a toll on their relationships. To think that such behavior will be forgotten and forgiven is unrealistic. Trust me, people will tell you they accept your apology and they are ready to move on but they won't forget.

THE PHYSIOLOGY OF ANGER

Anger is also physiologically harmful. Researchers have measured the effects of anger by asking couples to discuss an issue on which they disagree. While they are engaging in this discourse the couples have their vital signs, such as blood pressure and heart rate, monitored frequently. Even though the couples may appear calm on the outside, they are under measurable stress because their blood pressures and pulse rates increase dramatically during the discussion of the argument. Periodic high blood pressure is nothing to take lightly, but continual high blood pressure is a serious health condition. It can cause a wide range of medical problems such as heart disease and stroke.

Anger also interferes with the body's ability to fight off infections by weakening our immune system. The same researchers took blood samples from the couples during the reenactment of their disagreement. The samples taken during the discussion gave evidence of a suppressed immune system. When valuable psychic energy is spent being enraged about something, valuable physiologic resources that normally work to protect and enhance our health are being exhausted. As a result of our weakened immune system, we are more likely to become sick.

THE NEUROLOGY OF ANGER

Anger's effects on the brain are also well documented. Anger is produced deep in the brain in a structure known as the amygdala which is part of the limbic system. The limbic system has numerous connections with the frontal lobes which control higher level thinking. When a person becomes angry, the limbic system "overrides" the frontal lobes making rational thought difficult, if not impossible. It is only after this excitation in the limbic system has subsided that a person can act in a thoughtful manner.

A few weeks ago my wife and I were going out to dinner on a rainy evening. We were headed to a new restaurant and were unfamiliar with the route. By mistake I attempted to get into a left turn lane in an intersection where there was no turning lane. Oops! I was in the lane where the cars heading in the other direction usually can be found (if some confused psychologist hasn't mistaken it for a left turn lane!) When I realized the predicament I was more than a little concerned. I was never a great success in physics but I was certain that two solid masses could not occupy the same space at the same time. My wife started to scream at me at this inopportune time and I proceeded to tell her to, "Shut the hell up!" Double oops!! Needless to say, Polly didn't appreciate the way she was talked to. She didn't hit me but in a way I wish she had. Believe me, I paid for that grievous error for a long, long time. It was definitely a case of my frontal lobes taking a short vacation.

ANGER AND SUBSTANCE ABUSE

Anger can also contribute to alcohol and drug problems. Another study conducted using 1800 Western Electric workers in the late 1950's found that hostile/angry individuals were much more likely to use alcohol in excess and smoke cigarettes. The researchers theorized that individuals who have anger problems find a way to medicate themselves, in this case by drinking and using drugs.

HOLD IT IN OR LET IT OUT?

Many believe it is best not to repress anger or "hold it in." There are numerous mental health professional encouraging people to "get it out of your system" and "blow off some steam." The problem with this approach is that *the body knows no difference between anger repressed and anger expressed. Both cause the same physical and psychological reactions.* Whether you swallow it or scream it out, the anger is still causing problems with your health.

Those who encourage the expression of anger to relieve the problems anger causes may be doing everyone a disservice. Venting your anger to get rid of angry feelings has the opposite effect: it makes people *more* likely to be angry. Research over the past 25 years has clearly shown that expressing anger only increases the chance of getting angry in similar situations in the future. ANGER BREEDS ANGER.

What does that say about the counselors who run around with soft bats and pillows encouraging their clients to "get it out?" To say it nicely, they are misguided. We are concerned with teaching you HOW TO AVOID BECOMING ANGRY IN THE FIRST PLACE. That's the goal worth working towards.

THE DEADLY ENEMY INSIDE

Even if you can overlook all the regrettable events and embarrassing incidents that occur while you are enraged, there is another reason to learn to control your anger. Your anger could be killing you. A longitudinal study that tracked individuals over a twenty-five year period produced some very sobering results. In the late 1950's, medical students at the University of North Carolina took a test called the Minnesota Multiphasic Personality Inventory (MMPI) which contains a hostility scale. Years later researchers followed up with these individuals and found some very alarming trends. Of the doctors who scored in the top quarter of the class on the hostility scale, 20% were dead. Only 4% of the doctors in the bottom three-quarter of the hostility scale were deceased. Most died of coronary heart disease or stroke which gives credence to what Confucius said many years ago, *"You are not punished for your anger, you are punished by your anger."* So if you don't want to learn to control your temper for your spouse, your children, and your friends sake, do it for yourself. You'll not only be happier, you'll live longer.

Learning how not to become angry is like any other skill. It requires a change of values, a modification of your beliefs and the courage to take responsibility for your feelings. Besides, you don't want to let these difficult parents continue to ruin your days and nights, do you? That's like letting them win...even when they aren't making sense.

The techniques needed to bring about these changes can be learned with determination and a lot of practice. This is especially true since anger has been experienced throughout life, thus, you will be trying to overcome a habit that you've had for a long time. To make matters worse, the thoughts that produce anger usually occur at a level below our awareness.

The following example will illustrate how our thinking causes anger. Let's pretend a fictitious character called Bob has had some difficulties with a family. The child in this family was diagnosed as ADHD. There had just been a special education referral and the child qualified for special educational services as other health impaired (OHI). Bob had been involved with this case from the start and convinced the classroom teacher to let the student take his examinations in the special education resource room. Bob had to work very hard to get this teacher to make the accommodation. He was feeling good about the results of the evaluation and placement. Then he gets a letter in the mail from the parent's attorney asking (make that demanding) that the school pay for a lap top computer so the child doesn't have to rely on his weak handwriting skills.

Bob is enraged. He thinks, "How dare they! Now they must want a pound of flesh as well. They have no damn right to harass hard working people like me. Don't they know they're putting me in a very bad position. The superintendent is never going to go for this." It should come as no surprise that Bob's thoughts will produce anger.

But what exactly is it about these beliefs and evaluations of the letter that brings about anger?

Whenever you find yourself becoming angry you can be certain you are demanding something. In this case Bob was demanding that the parents not ask for a lap top computer. He was demanding he get what he wanted. He was ordering the universe to get in line with his requirements, which is about as grandiose as it gets. When his demands weren't met, he made himself angry. It's that simple.

There is one slight problem with making demands such as these: BOB DOESN'T RUN THE UNIVERSE. Parents have the right to act insensitively if they chose to do so. As much as we may dislike it, the law guarantees certain rights. Even if the law didn't grant these privileges, they would still be allowed to act badly because we all have free will. This right doesn't come from any department of education, it comes from a higher power still...the department of human nature!

To illustrate how changing what you think will change how you feel, consider this alteration to the above scenario. Rather than demanding the parents treat him fairly, Bob could think, "I really wish I was finished dealing with these parents. I wish they'd leave me alone but I'm obviously not the one who decides these matters. While they may be making a ridiculous request, they have the right to act ridiculously. **How else should difficult parents act other than like difficult parents?"**

The difference between these two sets of beliefs is the first one is an absolute demand and the second is a preference. We run into difficulties when we make commandments as if we were some type of god. Simply because Bob wants the parents to leave him alone (a god-like command) does not mean they will. Those who struggle with anger need to keep in mind a little secret...we can't get what we want just by demanding it. Insisting the parents do Bob's bidding is akin to demanding it rain tomorrow. He has approximately the same amount of control over each.

ANGER'S TARGETS

Anger can be thought of as resulting from the demanding core belief, "Things *should* be as I want them to be." This belief produces anger that can be directed at a number of people or situations such as:

1)   Anger at others
2)   Anger at self
3)   Anger at the world

ANGER AT OTHERS

It probably comes as no surprise that educators find it easy to make themselves angry at parents, colleagues, and students. Anger occurs when others a) block us from achieving our goals; b) attack our values; and c) threaten our well-being.

Anger from Blocked Goals

Mr. Settles, an assistant administrator in charge of discipline (i.e., the hanging judge), had recently suspended a sophomore for continually refusing to obey the requests of teachers and other school personnel. Mr. Settles wanted to deliver a clear message to the student that he (the student) didn't run the school. Before suspending him, Mr. Settles had a long talk with the student and it seemed as though the adolescent was starting to get the point. The student was upset because he would have to miss a field trip the following day. "All the better," thought Mr. Settles. "Maybe now he'll see the light and change his behavior."

The next day the student's parents drove him to the field trip anyway just to undermine Mr. Settles' authority. He was very upset because the student seemed to be starting to come around. Mr. Settles thought, "If they want to have a juvenile delinquent on their hands, they ought to just continue undermining authority figures. Why do they have to be so stupid? Can't they see what we're trying to do?"

Anger from Attacked Values

Mr. Woolridge had refused to allow a student to attend a homecoming dance because the student was still suspended due an incident that occurred a week prior to the dance. If John had attended the Saturday detention, Mr. Woolridge would have cut him a break. However, John was a "no show" for the detention.

John's parents phoned the school after the discovered John would not be attending the dance. In the course of the conversation they referred to Mr. Woolridge as a "Nazi" and the school as a concentration camp.

At that point Mr. Woolridge completely lost his composure and made some rather unprofessional remarks referring to the parent's intelligence quotient. The parents immediately called the district superintendent and sent letters to all the school board members. Mr. Woolridge will now be apologizing to the parents...in person.

We might all agree that it would be nice if parents weren't unreasonable but, as fallible humans, they have the right to be less than perfect. Demanding they be otherwise is invoking a god-like quality that will only upset us. Once again, demanding others do what we would like makes about as much sense as demanding it rain.

Anger from a Threat

After making a decision not to include an 8th grader in the new computer programming course designed for gifted children, Mr. Kingsbury picked up the local paper to find a very negative editorial written by the child's parents. Since Mr. Kingsbury was only a second year teacher he was not tenured and knew that these parents could create enough of a headache for his administrator that it may be difficult to have his contract extended.

The hardest thing for Mr. Kingsbury to accept was that he honestly believed the class would be too difficult for the child. He thought he was doing the child and parents a favor. "The hell with this," he thought. "The next time anybody wants to be in any class, I'll let them in and just flunk them. See how they like that."

Anger at Self

People become angry at themselves in much the same manner that they become angry at others. Instead of others breaking a universal commandment (such as "Thou shalt not drive below 65 miles per hour whilst in the left lane"), it is the individual who has broken a personal principle.

Anger at oneself can also lead to depression and feelings of guilt. People believe a) they have acted as they should not have and b) they are "rotten" for doing so. It is exactly this type of self-denigration that causes most depression. This makes sense when one considers the potential effects of an individual telling himself or herself, "I'm a no good jerk because I..." An individual could feel nothing but depressed if he or she was reindoctrinating himself with such a negative belief throughout the day?

Anger at the World

The final entry is somewhat of a catch-all. A certain percentage of individuals will be angry with nearly everyone and everything because the world is not the way they would like it to be.

As adults, we no longer hold our breath and throw temper tantrums, but the principles are still the same. Adults demanding a boss treat them fairly and the three-year-old holding his or her breath are both demanding that the world do their bidding. Lots of luck, by the way, with either an insensitive boss or the three year old!

INTERVENTIONS

Once again let me reiterate there is nothing wrong with anger per se. Anger is a normal human emotion. It can motivate us to act or it can be quite a destructive presence in our lives. It's what we DO with anger that matters most.

So how do we keep from letting anger cause physical, emotional, and behavioral problems in our lives? First, it is important to learn to listen to our self-talk so we can hear our demanding thoughts. Think back to the last time you were angry. Can you hear any SHOULDS, OUGHTS, HAVE TO'S, or THEY HAVE NO RIGHT TO'S in your thinking? More than likely one of these demands was there.

"He SHOULDN'T be such a jerk."
"Things HAVE TO BE easier."
"I MUST NOT be treated unfairly."
"He HAS NO RIGHT to do that."
"She HAS TO BE nice."

These demands can be examined to determine whether or not they are logical. Is there any evidence or proof that things have to be easier? Of course not. There is a *desire* that things be easier, but that holds very little weight in the overall scheme of things. Remember, we do not run the universe.

A very important change of values/philosophies occurred in my life that has allowed me to be much more at peace with the world. I have finally accepted the fact that **people are fallible and have the right to make mistakes**. The value I am speaking of is acceptance. Genuinely accepting others WITH their faults, inadequacies, and imperfections. This is easy to say but very difficult to live and I will be the first to admit that I fall woefully short at times...namely, the two weeks prior to spring break! We would be the first to complain if other expected continual perfection from us. Why expect it from someone else?

SWITCHING FROM DEMANDS TO PREFERENCES

The most important step in learning to control our anger involves changing a demand to a preference. If you can change "These parents SHOULDN'T hassle me" to "I WISH they wouldn't hassle me" you'll produce irritation instead of anger. Irritation is appropriate because it is moderate in its intensity. It isn't an overreaction. It's also logical since no one of sound mind would want to be involved with more difficulties. There are genuine hassles in life and it is appropriate to feel sad or irritated during those times.

TECHNIQUES FOR REDUCING ANGER

There are several techniques that may be helpful for changing your internalized dialogue from anger creating demands to preferences or wishes First, try to determine exactly what you are saying to yourself to produce anger. Hearing your internal thoughts may be difficult at first but you know what to listen for. Focus on the SHOULDS, OUGHTS, MUSTS, etc. Once you have your self-talk figured out, write it down. Now dispute this demanding thought by stating rational alternatives. For example, if your demand is, "These parents shouldn't be so demanding" you might counter that thought with:

1) "Where is the proof that these parents shouldn't be so demanding? Just because I want them to be a certain way doesn't mean they have to be that way."
2) "Rather than demanding they change maybe I could stop believing they have to change. It might be easier to accept their insensitivity as one of their undesirable traits and stop being obsessed with it."
3) "There is absolutely no reason why these parents have to treat me any differently than they are treating me right now."

It is also possible to use a tape recorder and record the demand. After the tape has played the irrational demand you can say a rational alternative. For example:

TAPE: My class size can't be this high...it is not fair!

VOICE: It may not be fair but it is the way it's going to be. My class size will be as high as it will be. Getting mad about it will change my blood pressure, but certainly not much else.

ANGER CUES

Many people tell me they remember these ideas *after* they've been angry. Obviously, by this time, it is too late. Learn to pay attention to the internal bodily signals that are appearing just before you get angry. Your jaw may tighten, nostrils flair, your stomach may churn, and you may feel hot all over. These cues can serve as a reminder to calm down, or as the kids say, "Take a chill pill."

For example, as you start feeling yourself become angry when you notice that the person in front of you in the express lane has more than ten items, you can 1) ask the offending party if she realizes this is the "express lane" (hint, hint) or you can 2) immediately use your rational coping statement. ("Some people act like insensitive jerks. Getting angry about it will probably only ruin my day.") Learning your own internal signals can be helpful in this regard.

Please don't confuse anger management with "becoming a door mat." Don't let people walk all over you. There's nothing wrong with calmly reminding the person abusing the express lane that ten items is the limit. Realize he or she can tell you to mind your own business or go to hell but at least you can feel as though you made an effort.

RATIONAL-EMOTIVE IMAGERY

Another technique that can be very effective is Rational-Emotive Imagery (REI). To learn REI you first need a quiet place to practice where you won't be disturbed. Start by imagining, as vividly as possible, the situation where you find it easiest to anger yourself. Mentally re-create this situation in terms of the setting, who was present, what sights, sounds and even smells were in the immediate area. Once you've imagined the situation as vividly as possible allow yourself to become as angry as you were when this situation actually occurred.

After 30 to 60 seconds of being angry, try to calm yourself down. Keep imagining the situation but work to reduce your anger. Once you've managed to think about the situation and stay only irritated rather than angry, try to discover what you told yourself to diminish your anger. Write down exactly what you said to yourself to accomplish this reduction of anger. This calming thought is your rational coping statement. Practice, practice, practice this thought until it becomes ingrained in your mind. It is this statement that will keep you from becoming enraged when things don't go the way you would have liked.

It is a good idea to practice this coping statement several times a day. Write it down on index cards and keep it in locations where you will see it throughout the day. You can practice this rational coping statement almost anywhere (especially when you're stuck in traffic).

If you find that you continually make yourself angry at a particular person or event, do some preventative work by using REI on that situation before you become enraged. Two or three times a day, vividly imagine the situation and let yourself become angry. Then use your rational coping statement to calm yourself. By rehearsing before hand, if and when you find yourself in the unpleasant situation, you won't be as likely to make yourself angry.

Ask yourself a few very important questions.

> Is anger helpful in my life?
> Does it enhance my health and happiness?
> Does anger allow me to experience the emotions I want to feel?
> Is anger helpful in my relationships with others?
> Does anger represent values I wish to embrace?
> Now for the biggy...Am I willing to work at giving up my anger?

If so, the techniques listed above will put you well on your way to reducing anger's negative effects. It all comes down to accepting the fallibility of parents and the unfairness of our world. People have the right to be wrong and the world doesn't seem to care whether or not we are treated fairly. This is not a tragedy, just a reality.

TECHNIQUES FOR REDUCING PARENTS' ANGER

Now we are on the other side of the coin...the side of where the child's parents are fantastically upset with you or the school. How do we deal with this scenario? Some suggestions.

First off...pick **your** time to deal with it (if this is possible.) One Friday afternoon around 4:00 p.m. I received a message that a certain parent wanted me to return her call. I was tired (as we all tend to be by late Friday afternoon) but I thought I might as well give this parent a call to be over and done with it.

To make a long story short, that was a bad idea. The parent was upset with me about something and I didn't have the patience to listen to her nonsense. I would have had the patience to put up with her complaint at 10:00 a.m. Monday morning but instead I argued with her. We both ended up in a bad mood and she wrote a letter to my boss tattling on me for being a bad boy (which we all got quite a chuckle out of later). Fortunately, my boss knows I'm a nice guy 99% of the time and if I did something objectionable it was probably only after being annoyed to within an inch of my life. Still, I let *her* control how *I* felt. How stupid is that! In my personal list of "The 100 People I Never Want to Control My Life" this parent came in # 1. And here I was letting her control my emotions...in a word, stupid.

HOW ONE QUESTION CAN CHANGE A MEETING

This next technique was gathered from one of my principals, Sue Alexander, who has an amazing ability to use language to bring about the desired results from a parent meeting. Mrs. Alexander is one of the best I've ever worked with when it comes to handling difficult meetings.

A parent came to her office one day and was quite upset about a situation involving his daughter. He spent a couple of minutes voicing his displeasure when Mrs. Alexander asked him a question, "Are you here to discuss this situation or are you just here to vent your frustration?" That question spoke volumes in a very subtle, but firm manner.

First, it brought to the parent's attention that he was carrying on a bit too much. The question could make the parent aware of Mrs. Alexander's covert message (i.e., calm down a bit) without having to come out and directly say, "Get a hold of yourself."

Secondly, it encouraged the parent to set aside his anger to focus on the problem at hand. It promoted a positive use of the meeting time rather than an unproductive bitch session. Sure, the parent probably felt good venting but it put a limit on the complaining.

Mrs. Alexander said the meeting took a new direction following this query. This seems to be a great use of language to bring a meeting back on track. Of course the parent could have said, "I'm just here to vent," but that is unlikely. If it became clear the parent was only interested in venting you can then attempt to keep the meeting to a reasonable length.

THE POWER OF TOUCH

Another tip that seems to work wonders (and I must be honest that I got this one from my older and richer brother John, a dentist, who probably has more people who dislike him as a dentist than people who dislike me as a psychologist) has to do with making physical contact with the parent. By physical contact I do NOT mean putting a forearm to the parent's ribs...try a handshake first. Any type of physical contact seems to somehow diffuse the situation. It's almost like the energy gets drained out of them.

THE PHANTOM MEETING

A tried and true classic is called the "phantom meeting." Occasionally a parent is reading me the riot act about something. We all get that from time to time. I don't know about you but I've never felt like I make enough money to take a lot of grief from parents. The day that I start making $150,000 a year I'll listen to any and all complaints but until that time I will put a limit regarding the amount of grief I will put up with. When I reach my limit I magically have a meeting to attend at another building (even when I don't). Boom... I'm out the door or the phone is hung up. This one never fails. When you do call the parent back a day or two later he or she has to be in at least a little bit better mood.

Finally, if all else fails (which it occasionally does) remind parents why you are in your chosen profession. There was a parent who had a wheelchair bound student in our high school. My guess is she had been fighting for this child his whole life and viewed every school employee as someone she had to confront to ensure his needs would be met. She came into school and was mad as hell because I asked her to fill out an adaptive behavior scale on her mildly mentally handicapped son. I tried to explain to her that the completion of this form was required by the state special education statutes. She had never been asked to fill out such a form and was upset by some of the questions.

After about ten minutes in my office I turned around to see if I had any of my butt left. I was about to head out the door to a phantom meeting but I thought I'd try one last time to get through to this parent. I said, "You know I think you are forgetting something here." She said, "What's that?" and I said, "**I'm not the enemy. Honestly, I'm one of the good guys.**" I told her I could have done anything I wanted to make a living. I chose to work with kids because this was what I wanted to do. Why would I do anything to insult her or her son?

At that point you could literally see the anger leave this parent. She was quiet for a moment and then apologized for being so angry but she just didn't understand why she had to complete the form. I explained it to her again but this time she was really listening. Two minutes later she was smiling and realizing I really *was* on her side. She went on to view me as someone she could come to with questions, who would be a source of support for her and her son.

One last point that is perhaps the most important. The difficult parents that we encounter everyday have already cost us several layers of stomach lining. Some have taken away a lot of our valuable time and energy. Ask yourself one final question: Do I really want to let them control how I feel, too? I can't speak for you but I don't want to give difficult parents anything more than they are entitled to and they do not have the right to control how I feel.

Remember, to expect a difficult parent to act like a role model...now that's CRAZY. Of course they are going to be difficult, that's why they have kids who are difficult. To expect any different is insanity on our part. Your real challenge is to accept the reality of the situation and become absolutely committed to NOT letting difficult parents ruin your day.

Chapter 7

COPING WITH THE ANXIETY

G iven the legitimate influence parents have today regarding the education of their children, it only makes sense to be aware of and respect their power. To be unimpressed by their authority is to dance in a minefield in the dark with sunglasses on...no matter how lucky you are eventually, boom.

I've observed a lot of administrators and teachers counting on luck to keep them out of trouble. Occasionally my district has a toe in the "gray area" of educational law but some folks spend all their time clearly supporting an untenable position (i.e., "No we won't make the bathrooms wheelchair accessible." "Just because your child's last teacher modified assignments doesn't mean I'm going to." "Our district doesn't have a physical therapist so even if you get a doctor to prescribe PT, we still won't have to give it to you.")

If you recognize any of the above "invitations" to a due process hearing and perhaps law suit, go ahead and feel very anxious. I won't try to dissuade you in any way, shape or form. When you are in clear violation of education law, the only rational feeling to have (if you're not severely psychotic) is some form of anxiety or fear. But let's define our terms before we get too far along.

FEAR VS. ANXIETY

It is important to point out that anxiety and fear are different emotions and will not be used interchangeably. **Fear** is an emotional response to the threat of harm, injury, or loss. **Anxiety**, on the other hand, can be defined as an emotional response to *perceived* dangers that seem real but which are mainly imaginary because so little probability of occurrence exists.

The important question then becomes, "What are the chances of the feared event occurring?" If you lay awake at night afraid a family filled with lawyers and a handicapped child will move into your district, you are probably experiencing anxiety. On the other hand, if you are constantly uptight because you know you're in violation of the law...that's fear. Chances are pretty good that sooner or later you're going to get nailed.

It is one thing to have a sense of anxiety regarding a situation, such as going to the doctor's office, but it seems a lot of people are experiencing a free floating sense of anxiety. That is, they constantly feel something catastrophic is about to occur. The feeling does not appear to be related to any one situation or event but is more of a general sense of foreboding. Such feelings are stressful and drain the body/mind of energy that could be used more productively.

THE ANXIETY OF ADOLESCENCE

Working with children and adolescents has become increasingly stressful in the past few years. If you need evidence consider these statistics compiled by the Department of Justice:

- Approximately one third of all crime has been attributed to children under the age of eighteen.
- More than 1.5 million adolescents are arrested annually.
- Approximately 2,000 adolescents are arrested annually for murder.
- Approximately 34,000 adolescents are arrested annually for aggravated assault.

- The murder rate per 100,000 for white males was 3.8 in 1950. By 1988 it had risen to 7.9. For black males the murder rate for the same period rose from 58.9 to 101.8.
- Violence is now the leading cause of death for 15 to 34 year olds.
- Nearly 35,000 people died by gun shot wounds in 1992 in America. Japan, a nation with half as many citizens, had 74 death by guns. Sixty-seven of those deaths involved organized crime figures.

The financial strain of juvenile crime is staggering. Consider the following figures recently released by various government agencies:

- The estimated cost of youth violence is $18 billion annually.
- The average cost to treat a gun shot wound is $9600.

These statistics address violence in general. What about violence and crime within our schools? The following data were gathered as part of a national survey.

- Approximately 300,000 simple assaults were reported (80,000 with injuries) in 1996.
- Approximately 44,000 robberies were reported (8,700 with injuries).
- Twenty-six percent (26%) of students carry a weapon to school at least once a month.
- Twenty percent (20%) of teachers have either been assaulted or threatened with violence.
- For every gun in schools, there are seven (7) knives.
- The annual cost of school vandalism is in excess of one-half billion dollars.

THE CAUSE OF ANXIETY

Our conscience is given the important task of reminding and warning us when our behavior is inconsistent with our values. Mr. Conscience also taps us on the shoulder when our behavior is morally and ethically wrong (according to personal definitions). Given the above definition of anxiety (i.e., an emotional reaction to perceived dangers that seem real but are mostly imaginary) it would seem that anxiety is sent to help us stay out of trouble as well. While this may be true in some instances, by and large, anxiety has a profoundly negative impact on our lives.

Anxiety does not alert us when our behavior is inconsistent with our values, it just alerts us! The free float sense of anxiety mentioned earlier supports that contention. People don't know *why* they're uptight, they just feel it

By continually creating harmful emotions and heightened arousal, anxiety robs us of the opportunity to experience joy. The states of anxiety and joy are mutually exclusive. Have you ever met an anxious, yet joyful individual? Keep in mind that anxiety also leads to burnout.

BELIEFS LEADING TO ANXIETY

Anxiety comes from the irrational belief that if a particular event were to occur, the event would be horrible, terrible, awful, or catastrophic. Anxiety is produced by 1) anticipating an "awful" event, 2) by exaggerating the adverse effects of this event, or 3) by believing if the event were to occur, it would turn out to be the "worst thing imaginable."

Throughout this chapter I will use various examples to illustrate the points. By choosing these examples I have not covered all the possible anxieties but that's not the intent of this chapter. Readers are encouraged to apply the lessons learned here to their own circumstances. The concepts are applicable to any anxiety, as all anxieties are created by our thinking *about* events rather than the events themselves.

Let's start by examining a very common fear: the dreaded due process hearing (or substitute "a very bad parent meeting" if you prefer). Many are absolutely terrified at the thought of a due process hearing or bad parent meeting. Usually the anxiety is produced when people convince themselves the results of this hearing/meeting may be bad. Interestingly enough, this portion of their thinking is actually quite rational. The hearing *may not* go well. There is always the possibility of coming out on the short end of the due process stick. The anxiety producing portion of an individual's self-talk follows the rational portion. "We could look bad and lose this hearing (rational portion) and that would be terrible, awful, and horrible and I couldn't stand it." It is this second portion of an individual's self-talk ("that would be terrible, awful, and horrible and I couldn't stand it") that is irrational and is the cause of the anxiety.

When an individual defines something as terrible, awful, and horrible they may be believing that, "The event would be very bad" but the emotional impact of such words translates to, "This is worse than 100% bad. This event is the worst thing possible." Practically no event is the worst thing possible. Certainly no one has ever lost a life as the result of a parent meeting.

Keep in mind that nothing is 100% bad. No matter what the misfortune might be, there is always another event that could be worse or the event itself could be even more unfortunate. That is not to say losing a due process hearing would not be bad, and maybe even 99% bad, but it's not so bad that a person could not stand it.

An excellent technique for conquering anxiety is asking yourself, "What's the worst thing that could happen?" In the due process hearing, about the worst thing that could happen would be that you would loss the hearing. While this would not be enjoyable, it is certainly a part of life on occasions. Logically, everyone understand that losing the hearing would not be a catastrophe but emotionally, it still feels the end of all life as we know it. To my knowledge no educators have ever been put to death following a poor showing at a due process hearing or a lousy parent meeting...not even in Texas!

In the scenario of a very bad parent meeting, about the worst thing that could happen would be for a shouting match to occur. Even if this did happen (and I've been at a couple) would the world end? Of course not. Life goes on. You pick up the pieces and move ahead.

THE ELEGANT SOLUTION

Another technique that can help people rid themselves of anxiety is known as **the elegant solution**. Assume "the worst" does happen and this feared event really does occur. Why would it be so awful? Would it really be the worst thing imaginable? Would the event traumatize the individuals involved to such as extent that they would be unable to ever experience happiness again?

Let's take the example of being given a poor evaluation by an administrator. Let's use this example to diagram a model of problem clarification and resolution known as the ABCs. In this model:

- the "A" part stands for "what happened"
- the "B" part stands for "what you thought"
- the "C" part stands for "what you felt and did"

A - (what happened) Given a poor evaluation by a superior.

At point "B" (what you did) you could tell yourself, "This is horrible. This is the worst thing that has ever happened to me. I'll never be able to show my face around here again." Such a belief would produce feelings of anxiety, embarrassment, and humiliation at point "C" (what you felt). As a result of the evaluation you might also do something (the other part of C) such as tell off the administrator or fail to show up for work the following day.

It would also be possible to evaluate the event in a different manner. A more rational evaluation at point "B" could be, "Wow, that's unfortunate that I didn't get a positive evaluation. Maybe there's something here I can learn. Negative feedback is hard to take but at least I know where they want me to improve." The emotional reaction at "C" would be an appropriate feeling of regret.

When the irrational beliefs at point "B" are examined they obviously are exaggerations. Anxiety often accompanies beliefs that exaggerate the bad effects of an unfortunate event.

Most feared situations turn out to be much less painful than had been imagined. Just last week it was time to do our semi-annual parent-teacher conferences. The elementary principal was going to be out of the building during this time so she asked me to sit in on a couple of potentially difficult conferences. The teacher involved in one of these was really feeling very nervous. The teacher and I discussed my role in the meeting before hand over lunch in the faculty lounge. We seemed to have things figured out but then realized it would be difficult to explain my presence at the meeting. Why is the school shrink here? Do they think our kid is nuts? We went back and forth on the best approach and finally decided I would be in the hall, within ear shot, if any trouble arose.

When the day of the meeting arrived the teacher was extremely uptight about this meeting. Several of the staff met me and said, "Mrs. Smith seems really nervous. She's been asking if you were around."

To make a long story short, I went down to the designated area outside her room just as the parents were arriving. I made sure the teacher saw me and knew that I was right outside the door. As you may have already guessed, the meeting went beautifully. The areas of concern were not even discussed! Near the end of the meeting the father even talked about supporting the teacher more in the future. All that worry and dread was for naught.

It commonly occurs that when the big event does finally happen it's actually "no big deal." The person who was anxious regarding a blood test will often tell you they barely felt the needle and had no idea why they were so worked up about a little needle prick. It was the worrying and fretting about it for days and weeks that was difficult to handle.

"I-Can't-Stand-It-Itis"

When someone evaluates a future event and says, "I can't stand it" they are holding a belief that is patently false. This "disease" is known as "I-can't-stand-it-itis."

If your principal called you into the office and said the school board was unhappy with your work and they were going to conduct a performance review to determine whether or not you would be able to keep your job, could you tolerate it? Of course you could stand it because **you don't have a choice**. Wishing it were not so will have no impact on reality. You can't go back in time and undo the event. Like it or not, you will tolerate it.

It's also important to remember that no event is ever "the worst thing possible." Right now think of your own worst possible event. Once you've thought of it, try to think of something even worse. Usually, it's not hard. Things can always get worse. A father of a friend of mine used to say, "No matter what your situation, you can always find someone who is better off than you and worse off than you." He was a very wise man.

Rational-Emotive Imagery

Rational Emotive Imagery (REI), previously discussed in the chapter on anger, is a technique that can be very beneficial in anxiety reduction. The beauty of REI is that it allows you to experience a feared event, albeit only mentally. Performing the feared event in your head is almost as beneficial as actually being there.

When you are about to experience the feared event (i.e., the parent meeting from hell), do some deep breathing. Flooding your brain and body with oxygen has a calming influence which can reduce the feelings of anxiety. Three deep breaths will do the trick. When you exhale, imagine all the worry, dread, and anxiety leaving your body right along with the air from your lungs. Reread the notes on REI, if necessary, from the chapter on anger management.

TECHNIQUES TO HELP PARENTS
COPE WITH ANXIETY

I put this at the end of the chapter because I thought some of you may not have a strong desire to help parents feel more relaxed. If that's the case, skip ahead. If you do want to learn some "anxiety busters for parents" keep reading.

I can't imagine many situations more frightening than arriving at a room full of professionals who are all about to tell you bad things about your child. Yet, we invite parents into this lion's den everyday. There are a few things that can be done to help them feel more at ease.

First and foremost, try to keep the size of the meeting down. If you can run a meeting with four people why have seven there? More people makes for longer meetings and you probably hate meetings almost as much as I do. If there's one day a week that I leave work when my contract says I can, I consider that a good week. Having several more professionals there, who all have to add their two cents worth, often makes for more laborious meetings.

Allow the parent(s) to bring a friend (as long as that friend isn't a lawyer or an advocate!) Of course we can't control who the parent(s) bring but I've seen may instances where a aunt or neighbor helps the parent(s) calm down.

Try to avoid jargon. Remember how you felt when your physician lapses into "doc speak" and you didn't have the faintest idea what the hell he or she was talking about. Save the jargon for your colleagues. I know it's hard. We all spent years learning how to use all those big words but give it a rest if you want to help the parent(s) feel at ease. If you have little or no concern for the parent(s), there are precious few ways to make them feel dumber than by using big words they don't understand...so fire away!

Ask the parent(s) a question or two at the start of the meeting so they will get the cob webs out of their throat. Once they hear their voice in the room they will be less anxious about asking questions and contributing to the meeting.

Speaking of questions, let them know it's okay to ask as many as they'd like. I always start the meeting by telling them I like to run these get togethers informally so if they have questions just ask them.

Tell parents the tried and true classic, "We may be experts in education but when it comes to your child, you know more than anyone here." Say this because it really helps parents feel at ease but realize that the sentiment expressed in the statement is often patently false. Sadly, educators often know children much better than their parents do because 1) we spend a lot more time with their child or 2) their kid will really talk to counselors but not to parents 3) we aren't blinded by several million years of evolutionary handy work making some parents incapable of accepting anything remotely negative about their child or 4) all, or any combination, of the above.

Lastly, and I'm being serious now, tell them we are here because we all want the best for their child. You can use my little speech about having the ability to have worked in any field but you chose education because you wanted this job. It's not copyrighted! That's a good one but your colleagues will probably bite holes right through their lips trying not to laugh. On second thought, maybe you should come up with your own little speech.

SUMMARY

Anxiety is caused by our beliefs, values, and evaluations about events and not parents, students or anything outside our bodies. Take comfort in the words of Marcus Aurleius, the Roman emperor, who nearly two thousand years ago said, *"If thou art pained by an external thing, it is not this thing that pains thee, but thy own judgment about it. And it is in thy power to wipe out this judgment now."*

Old Marc was right, you know.

Chapter 8

STRATEGIES FOR SUCCESSFUL PARENT CONFERENCES

A period of high stress for all educators is Parent-Teacher conferences. There is nothing quite like teaching all day and then facing the parents of kids you've just been in mortal combat with for the past seven hours. Can we all say "splitting headache?"

Most teachers start the meetings feeling tired and try their best to manage for the evening sessions. Some districts, like mine, are starting to also provide a day session for parents to come in because there are an increasing number of 2nd shift workers who are unable to make evening meetings. This has the advantage of letting the kids out of school for the day so teachers can rest up a little before the conferences.

The first advice is a no brainer...get some rest. As simple as this sounds it cannot be overemphasized. How many of us are better at handling difficult situations when we are rested? My guess would be 100%. When you know you've got a difficult couple of days ahead, do yourself a favor and get some extra sleep.

Not only will it make the parent-teacher conferences a lot more enjoyable in general but it will minimize the possibility of losing your cool with a difficult parent. When teachers (and people in general) are tired they are much more irritable and must less able to tolerate frustrating circumstances.

CALL FOR BACK-UP?

Another good idea is to ask an administrator or another supportive professional to sit in on the meeting(s) you think might be difficult. My principal has asked me to do this from time to time just to make certain things don't get out of hand. There have been times where I know if I had not been at a meeting to diffuse the situation, it would have been a very bad experience for everyone involved. I try to remain out of the conference unless I'm needed to step in and clarify a point or keep things moving along. The teachers usually just feel good knowing I'm there if needed.

There have also been times where I've gotten the distinct impression that having a male presence at a meeting has helped things go smoothly. Some fathers will think nothing of trying to bully or intimidate a female teacher but are less likely to engage in that kind of behavior with a male in the room. Please don't write me telling me I'm a sexist pig...I'm not. The sexist pigs in this scenario are the parents who engage in this type of behavior. I could be off base here but I know what I've seen during the meetings over the years.

Perhaps the most important thing is to have a plan for the meeting before you get in the room with the parents. Think about the kinds of issues that may arise and decide how you are going to handle them. Identifying the "hot" issues will probably not be too difficult. These are the problems that keep surfacing with the parents and child. Let me give you an example of an incident that kept coming up with a particular parent.

The child continually was tardy with his homework. The teacher's method of encouraging successful homework completion was to withhold recess time and allow the child to finish incomplete assignments while others were playing. Let me add that this meant the teacher didn't get a break to go to the lounge or make a phone call. This teacher was completely convinced that the kids needed to be held accountable for their behavior and the only way to turn around poor work habits was to apply a minor consequence when the child's performance was not up to par. The parent felt the teacher was picking on her child and had let the teacher know this through a series of nasty notes during the first nine weeks of school. Chances were pretty good that this issue would be a hot one during the conference.

The teacher thought about and planned how she would respond to the mothers complaints before hand. She told the parent that her child's academic skills were below where they could be and he needed to catch up before entering middle school. She believed the only way to help this child was to be kind but firm and make certain he will be held accountable for all missing work. In short, she communicated that she cared about the child and her motives were out of compassion and concern and not anger or revenge.

The mother was able to see that the teacher was doing what she, as an educator, believed was right for the child. They agreed to work together more in the future to make certain the student didn't start sliding again.

It's also very important to be positive with the parents. Remember, this child is the apple of their eye even if he or she is driving you crazy. Parents have a much better time listening to negative news if they hear something positive first. The key here is making sure they listen, not just hearing. Those of you with children, how do you feel when somebody criticizes your child? It's pretty difficult to listen to, isn't it? In your own life, who are you more likely to listen to and trust, a teacher who appears to dislike your child or a teacher who is fond of your child but has concerns for his or her education?

Please don't misunderstand what I am saying. Never tell a parent, "Everything is going fine" if that is not the truth. This is the time to openly communicate your concerns and enlist them in your plan to help the child. If you have some major concerns, you have an ethical responsibility as a professional to share your concerns with the parent. Anything less would be dishonest and not in the best interests of the child.

SANDWICHES

You can, however, pick the appropriate time and place to discuss your concern. One of my old professors from graduate school said something regarding this situation that I'll always remember...S_ _ _ Sandwich!

By S_ _ _ Sandwich, he was referring to the practice of sandwiching the bad news between two pieces of good news or affirming qualities about the child. Let me illustrate how the techniques works first by giving you the straight S_ _ _ and then the recommended S _ _ _ Sandwich.

Here's the Straight version. "Mr. and Mrs. Jones, thanks for coming in to meet with me. I've been looking forward to this meeting because I'm concerned about Johnny. He's missing a lot of school and it's going to be hard for him to catch up."

Now, the Sandwich. "Mr. and Mrs. Jones, thanks for coming in to meet with me. I've been looking forward to this meeting. Let me first say that Johnny is a great kid. He's funny and his classmates like him. He's great to have in class (bread). However, I am concerned that he's been missing too much school. It's starting to become difficult for him to make up the work (S_ _ _). He's such a bright kid I'd hate for him to fall behind (bread)." See how it works?

Which approach is going to bring about the results you'd like? The chances of the parents being an ally rather than an enemy are increased by the latter approach. I realize the example was a wee bit trite but I hope you get the picture.

I can hear some of you thinking, "That's too simple. Parents aren't fools. They'll see through such a simple ploy." This technique does work quite well with a majority of parents. Give it a try and find out for yourself.

WHAT PARENTS GO THROUGH

Keep in mind what the parents may be experiencing as well. If school hasn't been a successful experience for their child they are more than likely frustrated and sensitive to criticism. Recall the analysis of difficult parents earlier in this book. A fair percentage of parents over identify with their children and anything that a teacher says that is not 100% positive will be viewed as a criticism. That's why it is very important to focus on the child's behavior, what the child is doing, rather than any broad strokes about the child. It's much better to say, "Sue doesn't always turn in her work on time" as opposed to "Sue's work ethic could use some improvement." The first refers to the child's behavior and the second caste dispersions about the child's character. They may not like hearing either but they will be much more likely to acknowledge the former than the latter.

During the conference try to remain unemotional if things start to get heated. It's important to keep your wits about you. When you get angry it is much more difficult, if not impossible, to think clearly. Also, some parents try to get a teacher into a confrontation because if they can put the emphasis on the school, it will stay off the child and their parenting. When they can get the teacher, administrator or support professional fuming mad, they have taken control of the meeting. Now they are setting the agenda and the school folks are dancing to their tune. I sincerely hope you don't run into too many of these parents because you will have a very difficult time working constructively with this type.

Finally, keep these meetings short and sweet. Our district has the philosophy for spring and fall parent conferences that if a problem can't be handled in the 20 minutes allotted, there needs to be a follow-up meeting scheduled. Parents usually understand that there are another set of parents coming in following their meeting and there is only a certain amount of time. It is a good idea to point this out to some parents at the beginning of the conference to keep things moving along rather than stuck on one issue or problem.

If all else fails, keep in mind these meetings will be over in a few hours. Keeping things in a short term perspective is sometimes the very best advice of all.

Chapter 9

HELPING PARENTS OWN THEIR RESPONSIBILITIES

I spend a lot of time in parent meetings. If you added up the time I have spent around a table with parents it would probably come to some ridiculously high number that would make my heart skip a beat so I'm tempted but I'm not going to do the math. I can confidently say the number would be somewhere between 1,000 and 1,000,000,000.

My guess is most of you spend a lot of time in meetings, too. Even if you are not a specialist, as a teacher you are probably spending more time in meetings today than five years ago. Due to the problems facing kids today, it's important to form allies with parents. Perhaps more important, we need to make sure the professionals in schools are working together for the benefit of the child.

The educational/child problems of today are much more complicated than a few years ago. It's not as simple as, "Jimmy isn't turning in his homework." Now it's, "Jimmy's mother called to say they have no place to sleep tonight and the car broke down again. Can someone get Jimmy to the doctor's today after school because the doctor isn't writing anymore prescriptions for Ritalin until she sees Jimmy? Steve, you can drive him? Great. How's his reading? Oh, before I forget, his father was paroled."

The stress of working as an educator can be overwhelming at times. If we don't have safety nets for ourselves, it's much too easy to become disenchanted, depressed, and burned out. One of the best ways of keeping this from happening is through the support of the "team" in your building.

THE TEAM

The team I am referring to may be a formal collection of professionals in your building or it may be just other teachers who can relate to your struggles. You may find comfort just being able to talk to the members of your grade level or department. From time to time, everyone could use an ear to bend.

Before we discuss what goes into a successful team let's spend a little time defining the concept of "team." The most important concept to keep in mind is **teams have a common goal. Without a goal a team is just a collection of people**. It is this goal that drives the team, not the other way around. There are no successful teams in which the members try to make the goals fit *their* needs. The goal is usually implicitly understood but that does not mean there should not be discussion of the team's objectives (but no mission statements...*please)*. The goal may or may not be clear to all members. Plus, the means of reaching the goal will also need to be agreed upon.

Keep in mind that teams take time, they don't just happen. Part of this time needs to be spent planning. A consultant who works with our school, Perry Breseman, has a great quote that is perfect for this scenario..."**Teams need to plan to succeed or they plan to fail**." No matter how talented the members, a team needs to spend time growing as a unit or their impact will be minimized.

In our district we have a "child study team" at the elementary that has developed into a fine tuned machine. I have also worked in districts where the team concept was a miserable failure. What factors bring about success and what predicts conflict and division?

Our team has a great deal of **mutual respect**. We believe in the skills each member brings to the table. This team is definitely synergistic (another big word I've been trying to work in) meaning the whole is greater than the sum of the parts. We know each other's strengths and we consciously play to those strong points.

Another factor in a successful team is **trust**. Each member knows they will be treated in a professional manner. There can be no game playing. A team without trust is a disaster waiting to happen.

The ability to be **open** with one another is also important if a team is to function effectively. Each member must feel comfortable voicing their opinion without worrying they will be criticized for their views. Leave the egos at the door please. And while we are at it, lets forget about the turf issues as well. We all share the same turf, which is the learner. Who ever has the best chance at being successful with an intervention ought to be the person responsible for carrying out that task. For example, if a parent contact is recommended to enlist support with homework completion, the team member who has the best relationship with the parent is the likely choice to approach the mother and father. You need to understand your team member's strengths in order to make the best choices regarding responsibilities.

FOOS-NOOP

I have a little sign that I carry in my brief case which is placed in such a location that it is seen every time I open the case. It is the words (or letters) **FOOS-NOOP** which stands for **Focus On Our Students, Not On Other Problems**. This little sign reminds me what education is all about...kids. There are times when it is possible to lose sight of the best interest of the students. A good team makes sure this doesn't happen.

Another technique to keep yourself kid centered is pretending the student in question is *your* child. What would you recommend if this was your child? We had a difficult decision to make about a first grader who had not had a good year. The parents and classroom teacher were wondering whether or not retention might be the best decision. We really struggled with the pros and cons of retention for this child. We retain very few kids but this was a case where repeating a grade may have been the best decision. While I was thinking about the child I thought to myself, "What if this was my child? Would I want him retained?" My answer was an immediate,

"No." It finally came down to the fact that while retention may be beneficial, it was not the answer in this case. Plus, the risks of retention outweighed the potential benefits. We may have made a mistake; only time will tell. At least we made the decision with the child's best interests at heart.

Finally, most teams need **administrative support**. When you think about programs in your school, generate a list of projects that did not have administrative support and were successful. It doesn't take too long to finish that list, does it?

When administrators get behind a program with action (not just words) the program has a much higher chance of being successful. I wish it weren't so but it is about that simple. When you are given time to meet and encouragement to grow as a team, things usually work out. This is not always true because some people are better at sabotaging teams than the rest of us are at building them.

Think of the teams you have been on that have not been successful. Which one of the above mentioned factors was missing? Was it a lack of trust and respect, or did turf issues get in the way? When we can't agree to work together we look like fools to parents. We need to work with each other so parents will work with us towards a common goal...educating the child.

I don't think any educator would disagree with that last statement. But it's easier said than done for a couple of reasons:

1) Often the goals of the parents and the hopes of the school are at odds. There can easily be honest disagreement over the best course of action for the child. Add a lawyer and you've got two chances for an amicable resolution...1) diddly and 2) squat.

2) The most common reason we see parents is because of problems. It would be nice if we had the time, and parents had the time, just to get together to congratulate each other on a successful year. Time, after all, is a valuable commodity.

It's up to us, as professionals, to make certain we use that time wisely. There aren't a lot of us standing around the water cooler and if there are, shame on you! Get in your car right now and drive to East Troy, Wisconsin and we'll put you to work. Most of our days start frantically and get progressively more chaotic until we realize it's nearly 5:00 p.m. and we were suppose to go home over an hour ago.

How Parents See Us

I submit to you this is not how most parents view educators. On some level they believe from the moment we arrive at school until the times comes to leave, we are concentrating on *their* child. Their universe is Bobby or Susan, and that's understandable.

Parents sometimes forget that the rest of the world doesn't revolve around their child. Being a parent, I can definitely understand. My wife and I also forget when we start babbling about our kids so I do understand. Moms and dads have visions of us sitting around the office thinking, "I wish they'd call because I am completely out of work. No other child has a need other than Bobby."

When we aren't in our roles as educators, we have the same type of distorted perceptions as parents. I was doing a seminar on stress management to a group of employees at a bank and they kept talking about all the stress they felt from their customers. The president of the bank said, "I might leave for an hour and have ten messages to return phone calls. Sometimes I just can't get back to people until the next day and they give me a hard time for not getting back to them right away. They must think I just sit around waiting for the phone to ring like their accounts are my only concern." It struck such a cord in me because I hear the same sentiments from school employees quite often. To tell the truth I've been one of those people who was mad when the bank calls back a day later. I always assumed they just sat around counting money.

GUILT REVISITED

Parents have very busy lives. Often they don't have the time (or won't take the time) to do the things we ask of them. This leads to the inevitable feelings of guilt. Needing to blame someone to displace these unpleasant emotions, the parents get angry with the teachers for not providing their children with a perfect education. Teachers get frustrated with parents for failing to be cooperative and sympathetic to their requests. RESULT: blaming, hurt feelings, and mutual dislike. SUFFRAGETTE: Child.

When you meet with the parents always, always, always acknowledge they are busy people, too, and thank them for attending the meeting. This is just a simple way of demonstrating their contributions are genuinely appreciated. Also, it demonstrates the respect they deserve.

THE AGENDA

One of the things I have learned over the years is to rely on an agenda to guide the meeting, especially with parents who like to control the course of events. The agenda can be short and even hand written but everyone at the table should get a copy.

An agenda allows you to keep the meeting focused. I know there are only one or two things in this lifetime that you enjoy more than being in a two hour meeting with parents **after** a hard day at work. Trust me when I tell you the agenda can keep things moving along rather than regurgitating the same points over and over.

An agenda allows you to deal with the topics in the order *you* choose. At a meeting with a parent to discuss the child's IEP, the mother kept insisting we get to the IEP before we had discussed the evaluation. We felt there were some important points in the evaluation that would support our position on the IEP so we wanted to bring those out prior to discussing goals for the next school year.

The mother kept trying to jump right to the IEP. I explained to her I thought it was a good idea to follow the agenda and that we would get to the IEP right after we finished going through the evaluation. She had no problem with this and really, what could she say? The next item on the agenda was the IEP. To make a long story short, we then had the opportunity to emphasize the school's position, which was not the mother's position. The IEP was written in a much more reasonable manner I believe as a direct result of the order of items on the agenda.

Some of you may be thinking, "But sometimes we aren't sure exactly why the parents want to meet. How could we have an agenda?" Your practice of having an agenda would require you to determine their reasons for requesting a meeting which would also allow you to prepare for the meeting in advance. This would cut down on the "ambush conference" in which parents surprise you by dropping a small bomb into your lap.

If they say, "I don't want to discuss this over the phone, I want to speak to you in person" you can always say, "I understand that but there might be other professionals who need to be here and I can't invite them unless I know a little bit about your reasons for getting together."

Reading over the last few paragraphs I could see where these techniques may appear to be "sneaky" but that's not the intent. I prefer to think of these techniques as means of making certain ownership stays with the appropriate individuals. Parents are masters at conning the school into owning things that are not our responsibility. And this is not only the parents fault...it's our fault, too.

THEY GIVE IT, WE TAKE IT

Others like to give ownership and teachers/educators like to take it. Let's face it, that's why we are in this business. We work with kids because we believe we can help. We believe the lives of children are important. Those two beliefs are the necessary ingredients. Add a pinch of "parental diffusion of responsibility" and we have ownership problems.

By diffusion of responsibility, I am referring to the fact that most parents who have ownership problems have a myriad of other difficulties as well. They have a habit of losing jobs, don't get along with their landlord, and always seem to have a car that breaks down. It's a good idea to give parents permission to leave those problems at the door when you get together with them.

When you are aware the parent has other issues that are also pulling at their concentration it's an excellent idea to say something like, "Right now we all need to focus on what's best for Bobby. Everyone in this room, his teacher, his principal and especially you, Mr. and Mrs. Smith, need to try to focus on Bobby's education. Can we all agree to come together for Bobby right now?"

WHAT'S OURS? WHAT'S YOURS?

As you analyze the situation, you need to be constantly asking yourself, "What do we own and what don't we own?" This is easy to say and obviously much harder to discern. Use these four questions as a guide:

1). What is the concern?
2). Who is responsible for the concern?
3). What can I do to assist _____ with his or her concern?
4). How do I keep from owning someone else's challenges?

Let's take a few examples that may help clarify this model. The first involves a handicapped child who was having difficulties forming friendships. Sara seemed to have a few playmates at school but her mother was bothered by the fact that none of those children wanted to come over to their house on weekends or stay overnight.

The child's mother wanted us to "make" other kids be friends with Sara which is not something we could do. Mrs. Smith was angry and felt like we weren't doing enough for the child.

1). What was the concern?
   Sara's lack of friends.
2). Who was responsible for the concern?

In this case, primarily the mother but also the school to a lesser degree.

3) What can we do to assist Mrs. Smith with her concern?
The school had made numerous recommendations to the parent for interventions that would improve the child's social skills. For example, we had encouraged the parent to have the child become involved with outside social activities such as Girl Scouts and summer recreation.

4) How do we keep from owning someone else's challenges?
The most effective thing we can do in this regard is to be very clear with the parent regarding the school's role. The goal of public education is, well, public education. We can not make other children want to go over to play with a specific child. Perhaps our biggest challenge was helping the mother see things in a rational manner. Her demands for other children to comply with her child's wishes were unrealistic.

We could have spent a lot of time and energy on this case. I've known other schools who might get into the business of calling other parents to ask if they would be willing to let their child visit Sara's home which would clearly be taking ownership for the problem.

The other point to consider has to do with the parent's capacity to be satisfied. Once you start owning this problem, what's to keep you from taking over other problems for this family? How long until you are driving the child to the doctor?

Let's look at another example. This one involves a child receiving tutoring after school. The mother drove the student to the location where the tutoring was to occur (a public library) but the student never made it into the building. He went in the front door and turned around and left.

1) What is the concern?
Student fails to attend tutoring session.

2) Who is responsible for the concern?
Clearly the student. (It wasn't as clear to the mother who was responsible.)

3) What can the teacher do to assist in the problem?
   Very little other than communicate to the parent if the
   student does not attend in the future.
4) How do I keep from owning someone else's challenges?
   This may seem like an easy one but in the past the parent
   would blame the school for not meeting the student at the
   front door or some other silliness and the teachers would
   engage in some debate with the parent.

This time the parent called the teacher for some other reason and
the teacher asked, "Where was Steve last night?" The mother
responded, "He was with you." The teacher said, "He never showed
up." At this point the mother was starting to get upset and said,
"That's impossible. I drove him there myself." The teacher
responded, "He never showed up in the library." After they figured
out what had transpired the teacher told the parent, "I guess you have
something to talk about with your son," said "goodbye," and hung up
the phone.

MEETING REVISITED

Let's get back to the meeting scenario for a minute. As was
stated, usually meetings are called because there is a problem. If a
problem is going to be eliminated or at least improved, there has to be
a plan of action. It is a good idea to have someone at this meeting to
be a recorder or note taker. Many times excellent plans are
formulated at these meetings but there is not a clear understanding of
who is responsible for each planned intervention.

I have been at meetings where there has been a concern that a
student may be having a vision or hearing problem. Someone
recommends making a referral to the school nurse who is not in
attendance. Everyone agrees that having a hearing and vision
screening would be a good idea but it is not clear who is responsible
for contacting the school nurse. The teacher assumes the school
social worker is going to contact the nurse and the social worker

assumes it will be the teacher's responsibility. In the confusion the school nurse is never contacted.

If someone is taking notes, the results of the meeting can be summarized before all parties leave. Copies can be made and handed out or mailed to the home. Such a form should contain the following information:

1). Student's name and grade
2). The date of the meeting
3). Who attended the meeting
4). The primary problems (only two or three)
5). Recommended interventions to correct the problem
6). Person responsible for each intervention
7). Follow-up date (when the team will meet or talk again to check on the student)

It only takes a few minutes and also documents that attempts are being made to meet the student's needs. Keep in mind, documentation is becoming increasingly important in this age of litigation. There are more parents who are suing school districts for failing to educate their children. The burden of proof is on the district to demonstrate that there were attempts made to make accommodations for the student. Documentation like this may keep your district out of a law suit or save the day if they ever find yourselves in one. This form can be modified in any number of ways to include other information that is of interest.

DOES THE STUDENT ATTEND THE MEETING?

An important decision to be made is whether or not the student should attend such meetings. There are two schools of thought on this question.

Some believe that since it is students who are most responsible, it is senseless to hold a meeting to discuss plans for students unless they are in attendance and are actively involved in the decision making (assuming they are not in kindergarten!). Others will argue that with students in attendance, teachers will be less than 100% honest, not wanting to hurt the students' feelings. Additionally, having students listen to teacher(s) describe their less than stellar performance in and of itself can be damaging to their self-confidence.

I have been at meetings where the teachers take turns explaining how poorly the students are performing and, as they go around the table, students becomes more and more distressed. Is this necessarily a bad thing? I don't think so. It needs to be made clear to the students that the intent of the meeting is to help them perform more effectively. Students may feel picked on but hopefully they will also gain a sense that teachers are concerned about their progress.

My solution involves a compromise: during the initial portions of the meeting it might be best not to have the student in attendance. It is true that some teachers, out of compassion, tend to minimize a problem not wanting to hurt the child's feelings. Having the student in the room during the problem identification portion of the meeting may cause some teachers to be less than totally honest. Therefore, I think it's best to not have the student in attendance during the first part of the meeting.

Once the information regarding the student's behavior and grades has been discussed and it's time to start formulating a plan, the student should be invited into the meeting. When the student enters the room I usually tell him or her, "Now we really need your help. You know we're here because things at school haven't been going as well as they could be. It's time to get back on the right track so we're going to work on a plan to help you get going again. We all want you to feel that this plan is fair because you have to be able to live with it. That's why we need you to help us out."

If a student doesn't feel a plan is fair, the interventions are probably not going to work. What seems fair to adults may seem totally unfair to kids. Also, by inviting the student to have input in the plan they gain a sense of ownership (hey, there's that word again).

A majority of these meetings are successful. If nothing else such a meeting demonstrates to the parent and child the school is concerned and willing to put forth time and energy regarding the student's education.

I've been at meetings where a parent first learns that a student has been marked absent eight times during first period. The parent knows that the student is leaving the house every morning at 7:15 a.m. but did not realize the child was not always making it to school.

KURT'S STORY

Another example of the ingenuity students can display is illustrated by Kurt, a fourth grade student. In a similar circumstance, Kurt was being reported tardy to school on numerous occasions. He walked to school and would simply take his time getting there so he would not have to sit through the first subjects of the day, math, which he disliked. After meeting with the father, who was concerned and willing to do whatever necessary, a plan was formulated that would have the father drive Kurt to school each morning.

Everyone left the meeting feeling very confident that the problem of tardiness was dealt with in a satisfactory manner. I wasn't so sure the father needed to drive the child to school because this was Kurt's problem not his father's but I bit my lip on this one. With his father dropping him off at the front door, how could Kurt keep missing math? Somehow the problem continued as two or three times a week Kurt would wander into class about forty minutes late. School personnel assumed that the father, for some reason, was not able to drive Kurt to school each day and, therefore, he was showing up late on the days he walked. It was almost by accident that the school found out what Kurt was doing to keep missing math class.

Kurt's father was driving him to school each and every morning. I was at school for an early meeting one day and saw Kurt come into the building ten minutes early. When I saw his teacher later that day I commented that at least Kurt was on time today. The teacher explained that Kurt was late coming to class that day as well. With some minor detective work the next day, we found out how Kurt had been keeping up this tardiness game. Kurt had been hiding in the last stall in the bathroom during first period math! He wouldn't do it every morning because he was smart enough to realize that missing each morning would probably mean a phone call to his father. He knew once the school and parent communicated they would realize something was wrong...all this from a fourth grader!

Now every once in awhile you'll run into a Kurt that is a good enough con man to get around all obstacles, at least for a period of time. This can be cut to a minimum if everyone is clear about their responsibilities after the meeting. Tell the parents exactly what you are going to do and then do it. Most importantly, make certain the parents are clear regarding their responsibilities and are committed to carrying them out as well.

The student will search the plan for the weakest link and that is where he or she will try to sabotage the agreement. Even though the student will usually have a portion of the plan to own, you can't *make* the student responsible. You can, however, convince the parent to hold the student accountable for his or her behavior.

You can't shackle the student in a desk but the school can file truancy charge and the parents can agree to let the consequences of skipping school fall squarely on the student's shoulders. You can't make the student complete assignments but you can inform the parents of their child's performance and help them see the importance of controlling the kids reinforcers (car, phone, allowance, etc.).

Finally, and this is sometimes the hardest step, you can accept the parent's right to refuse to do the correct thing. That's one of the great things about this country, you have the right to be wrong...case in point, Rush Limbaugh (or Bill Clinton if you please).

Helping parents accept ownership over problems implies that we can not pick up the ball if they refuse to take it. If the parent refuses to comply, the only wise thing to do is be responsible for your portion and work to get them to be responsible for their part. Yes, I know it's hard but unless you've got a big red "S" on your chest and a cape on under your clothes, it's the only option that's feasible.

Chapter 10

MORE STRATEGIES FOR DEALING WITH DIFFICULT PARENTS

When dealing with difficult and potentially hostile parents on educational issues, you've got several options to consider. You can a) give in to the parents' requests, b) hold your ground and risk a due process hearing, or c) negotiate and try to find a compromise both sides can live with. The pros and cons of each of these alternatives will be examined in turn.

As has been discussed previously, parents have a tremendous amount of power, especially if their child has been diagnosed as having a special educational need or as eligible for modifications under Section 504. They can demand the sun and settle for the moon. It is essential that you know if the law grants these parents the capacity to receive the modifications they are requesting. You will certainly want to know this before the dispute goes to a hearing. That's where a good lawyer (excuse the oxymoron) comes in handy.

WHEN TO CALL THE LAWYER

Hopefully your district has a lawyer on retainer that has experience working with education law, special education and 504 processes. As in any legal practice, the more cases the lawyer has handled the better versed he or she will be in the court's *interpretation* of the law. The interpretation is much more important than the actual wording of the legal statute.

As has been discussed, 504 law has been on the books for more than twenty years but has only recently been used in educational matters. The courts are in the process of interpreting the law and many educators are watching the outcomes of these cases in an attempt to determine the actual manifestation of the law. Said another way, educators are trying to ascertain how much static they have to tolerate before they tell certain parents and advocates to take the longest of walks on the shortest of piers.

FOLDING YOUR TENT

There appear to be a few situations in which courts have consistently ruled for the parents and against the schools. For example, if a child has been diagnosed as ADHD, the school is going to have a difficult time finding the child ineligible for 504 modifications. Even if you believe the child has been misdiagnosed or is not in need of the modifications requested, you'd be wise to swallow hard and accept this one.

Be aware, however, that there is a real danger in acquiescence. When you give in to difficult parents, some take this as a cue to ask for even more. Now you've given in to more than you feel is fair and they want additional changes.

AN IMPORTANT DISTINCTION

You need to be able to differentiate between the parents who genuinely feel their child is entitled to an accommodation because it is in the student's best interests from the parents who just enjoy being difficult. Here's a few helpful hints to keep in mind when you're trying to make this distinction:

Do the parents seem to be able to explain why they believe their child needs a particular accommodation? If they can rationally justify the need for say, shortened assignments, chances are they are genuinely looking out for their child. If they just insist that the school meet their demands, you're probably dealing with parents who enjoy being tyrants.

Are they willing to help with their child's education outside of school? If so, these are most likely parents who are trying to be advocates for their children. I get very suspicious of parents who demand accommodations but won't lift one finger to try and help the child at home. If the child's best interests were really at heart, they would be willing to role their sleeves up and demonstrate their concern.

Have these parents unfairly criticized the school in the past? You know the parents I am referring to. No matter what schools do there are a small percentage of parents who will be dissatisfied and expect the schools to do more, do it better, and with less money. If the parents have been supportive in the past but disagree over the plans you suggest for their child, their concern is probably out of genuine disagreement with the plan and not as a vendetta to get back at educators.

Are the parents willing to come in and discuss the situation informally or do they want to proceed with advocates and lawyers from the very beginning? Most reasonable parents try to work out problems through the easiest, most direct route to start with and don't escalate the proceeding until they feel they have no other choice. There are some parents who literally will not sit down to chat without a parent advocate at their side. The battle lines are drawn from the moment there is a disagreement on the needs of the child.

THE DUE PROCESS HEARING

What happens when the parents threaten with a due process hearing? Usually, nothing. An overwhelming majority who threaten to call for a due process hearing do not follow through on the threat. When they find out the hassle involved, they try to work things out without going to a hearing or legal suit.

I have been involved in a couple of cases where the school has brought a due process hearing against the parents! One case involved a child whose parents kept demanding more and more accommodations. We tried to satisfy the parents but it soon became apparent that this was not possible unless we provided a full time tutor for their child.

When the district hired a new superintendent, one of the first things he did was discuss this case with me. When I explained all we had done previously and what the parents still were demanding, he said, "That's ridiculous. Draft a letter and tell them there is no way the school is going to grant their request and that we will be asking for a due process hearing so they can see once and for all we are not responsible to meet every demand they can come up with." I could have kissed him.

Guess what? After the school "called their bluff" the parents became a lot more reasonable in their requests. I liken this situation to a child who is looking for limits. The child becomes more and more obnoxious as if to say, "Isn't somebody going to stop me?" Well, parents need to hear "no" once an a while, too.

WINNING THE DUE PROCESS HEARING

DO NOT plan on winning a due process hearing unless you have documented everything you've done. Leave a paper trail of everything you do for the child. I know you've heard it a hundred times but it's true.

Also important is writing down any phone conversations you have with the parents. It doesn't have to be typed or on letterhead stationary, just scribble down what you talked about and make sure the date is noted as well.

Most of you have probably learned the importance of documentation the hard way...by getting burned. One of the things that separates us from our animal relatives is the human capacity to learn without directly having to experience an event. Please make good use of that potential and learn to write things down before you wind up with your behind in a sling. Because sooner or later, it will happen.

You usually get burned by parents you trust completely and that's why it happens! There are some parents who have trouble written all over them. These are the parents who come into school with a list of demands for their son or daughter. It couldn't be any more apparent these parents could be trouble if they had flashing lights spinning around on top of their heads. Naturally you cover your behind with these parents and leave a paper trail....you'd be a fool not to.

THE WOLF-PARENT IN THE SHEEP-PARENT CLOTHING

The ones who nail you are the ones who seem so nice. Then you think, "Oh, they won't care if we change this IEP without contacting them first. I'll give them a call later on to let them know what we're doing." (Famous last words.)

I hate to sound paranoid but it is true that you really can't be certain of anything or anyone these days. People are not who (or what) they seem. If you get in the habit of doing things the right way (i.e., documenting, following procedures) all the time, you'll never have to worry about who might be ready to catch you cutting corners. It's much, much better to take your time and not take short cuts when working with parents because, sure enough, eventually you'll run into a lawyer or advocate in parent clothing.

If you're like most of us and are going to cut corners, at least do it in a way that will benefit kids. For example, we occasionally will bring a kid into a special education classroom for a short period of time to get the kid some help even if they do not qualify for special education services. If we got caught we'd be in some trouble but I'm hoping the slackers at the Department of Public Instruction never read this book. (And if they do, I'll swear I made this whole thing up just to illustrate the point.)

If we get caught, you can hang us from our thumbs. I'd never place a child in a program without talking to the parents first. If they say go ahead, it's worth the risk to us. The kids are a heck of a lot more important than the rules.

THE NEGOTIATIONS

If you decide to negotiate with parents, which is usually what happens, beware of one potential hazard....the dreaded **time suck**. By time suck, I am referring to the parents who suck up all your time as if you worked for their child exclusively. The truth of the matter is we work for a whole bunch of people's kids and those other parents expect us to do things for their kids, too.

The worst time suck I've ever been a party to (and believe me, it was no party) involved a case where we had ten (yes, that's right, 10) IEP meetings in one school year. Realize of course this doesn't take into account the hours of meetings before the actual meetings to plan our strategy. Also missed is the time I spent on the phone with people from the state's Department of Public Instruction trying to get questions answered. At this point I was ready to give the parents the moon, sun and a time share on Mars just to be done with the endless meetings.

It's difficult to say who "won" this case. We didn't give in to their demands but I certainly didn't feel like the victor at the end of the year. I'd say both sides lost.

NEUTRAL GROUND

It might not be a bad idea to meet with the parents at some place other than the normal school setting. There have been times we've met with parents at a different location and it has seemed to change the feel of the meeting. The parents don't feel as threatened being out of the school.

DON'T RUSH

As busy as we all are, there are situations where things can't be resolved in an hour meeting. It's okay to table discussion for the time being and agree to get back together at a later date. This is especially true if the meeting is bogging down and you're not getting any movement from either side.

Keep the Numbers Down

As was stated earlier, one of my personal pet peeves is the meeting that has 127 people jammed into a room trying to all put their two cents worth. I hate it. **If people aren't absolutely essential in the meeting, they shouldn't be there.**

Let's say a child has a classroom teacher, LD teacher, ED/BD teacher, music, art and speech therapist. If the all the teachers have similar concerns, let the classroom teacher represent the entire group.

Think how the parents feel when the walk into a staffing and there are 127 of us around the table with our pads of paper and pens. Now there will only be 121 and I think you'll admit that's at least *less* than 127. But you get my point, I hope.

Too many cooks spoil the soup (or something like that) and the same is true for school meetings. Realize there will be teachers offended that they weren't invited but these are teachers that probably need offending. It always amazes me there are people who **want** to be at these slow motion train wrecks! My whole career I've been ducking as many of these meetings as I can and there are people mad at me to this day because I told them it would be better if they could just sent a written statement rather than attend in person. The brilliant author Oscar Wilde (no relation) once said, "*There are two great tragedies in life. One is not getting your heart's desire and the other is getting it.*" That doesn't sound quite right but it's close.

Stay Calm

This one has been stated earlier but it's worth repeating. Once you lose your cool, the chances of something constructive coming out of the meeting are slim. Try to remind yourself to stay calm. Give the parents a little extra grace for the sake of the kid. And, if the meeting disintegrates to a bickering session, you probably have to get back together with these same parents next week anyway so try to hang in there if possible.

KEEP YOUR EYES DOWN THE ROAD

One final point, keep in mind that decisions you make today with parents could have an impact on what occurs years later. Many of these parents belong to advocacy groups such as C.H.A.D.D. and when they have found that a school will give in on an issue they run back to their meetings to spread the word. Soon it seems as if the flood gates have opened and you get a lot of the same types of calls asking for the same types of modifications.

Plus, the modifications you make for a child in 2nd grade may be insisted upon by the parents years later when the accommodations are no longer appropriate. Always think about the repercussions your immediate decisions may have in the future. It's a shame educators have to be so preoccupied with this type of thinking but that's the kind of world we are living in. Your decisions are not made and carried out in a vacuum. Think "long term" before you act.

SUMMARY

1) Call the lawyer.
2) Know if you're in the right or wrong before you make any kind of stand.
3) Determine if the parents really believe their child is entitled to the modification or are they just being difficult.
4) Don't panic if they threaten a due process hearing or some other type of legal suit.
5) Document everything.
6) Worry about the parents you don't need to worry about!
7) Beware of the time suck.
8) Find a common ground and move ahead.